C000101146

Language and Culture

Papers from the Annual Meeting of the British Association of Applied Linguistics held at Trevelyan College, University of Durham, September 1991

Edited by

David Graddol
Linda Thompson
Mike Byram

British Association of Applied Linguistics

in association with

MULTILINGUAL MATTERS LTD

Clevedon · Philadelphia · Adelaide

ISBN 1-85359-207-2 (pbk)

Published by the British Association for Applied Linguistics in association with
Multilingual Matters Ltd.

UK: Frankfurt Lodge, Clevedon Hall, Victoria Road, Clevedon, Avon BS21 7SJ.
USA: 1900 Frost Road, Suite 101, Bristol, PA 19007, USA.
Australia: P.O. Box 6025, 83 Gilles Street, Adelaide, SA 5000, Australia.

Printed and bound in Great Britain by the Longdunn Press, Bristol.

Contents

Preface   v
Linda Thompson

Cultural Considerations in Linguistic Description   1
Gunther Kress

Culture is a Verb: Anthropological aspects   23
of language and cultural process
Brian V. Street

Discourse and Social Change in the Enterprise Culture   44
Norman Fairclough

Cultural Studies for Advanced Language Learners   55
Ana Barro, Mike Byram, Hanns Grimm,
Carol Morgan, and Celia Roberts

'I am a Creole, so I Speak English': Cultural   71
ambiguity and the 'English'/Spanish
bilingual-bicultural programme of Nicaragua's
Atlantic coast
Jane Freeland

Cultural Orientation and Academic Language Use   84
Lixian Jin and Martin Cortazzi

Projecting a Sub-culture: The construction of shared   98
worlds by projecting clauses in two registers
Susan Hunston

Developing Practices of Resistance: Critical   113
reading for students of politics
Romy J. Clark

'Song-lashing' as a Communicative Strategy in Interpersonal Conflicts in Yoruba Land: A sociolinguistic appraisal
Tope Omoniyi   123

What is the Russian for *Perestroika*?
Kay Richardson   133

Dialogic Relationships and the Construction of Knowledge in Children's Informal Talk
Janet Maybin   142

Preface

The 24th Annual Meeting of the British Association of Applied Linguistics (BAAL) was held at Trevelyan College, University of Durham between 13th–17th September, 1991. It brought together over 170 delegates representing not only diverse language communities, but diverse use within those communities. The congenial complementarity of the conference was reflected in the scope and range of the papers presented and in the more limited selection included in this volume here. The common bond is a shared interest in the conference theme: *Language and Culture.*

The papers included here have been selected for the diversity of perspective which they offer on the theme and for the ways in which they reflect current thinking on the interdependence of language use and situational contexts. At the micro-level this can be seen in variations in the individual's language use, as appropriate to social contexts and available audience. At the macro, societal, level it can be seen in the social events (such as 'lashing') which are culturally determined and specific.

The papers presented here also reflect current thinking on the sometimes subtle and sometimes not so subtle ways in which an individual's language use is constrained as much by extraneous factors such as social values and norms of behaviour as it is by the individual's linguistic repertoire. The knowledge gap experienced by individuals between knowing what to say but not being sure of when to say it is particularly transparent to observers. The conference brought together some of these observers who have enjoyed the privileged position of observing people using language. It is when the experienced watch the less experienced, child or foreign language learner, that the inadequacy of the purely linguistic description is most obvious. A comprehensive description of language use, by individuals in social settings, highlights the dual development of language and social cognition.

We do not claim that recognition of this interdependence is entirely novel. This collection is more a reaffirmation of the eclectic illumination offered by interdisciplinary descriptions of language use. At a time when subject boundaries are being redrawn and reinforced as devices of self-protection in the increasingly competitive world of research ratings, the suggestion of corporate effort may seem naive, but it existed at the conference and is reflected within this collection.

Linda Thompson,
University of Durham
June 1992

Cultural Considerations in Linguistic Description

Gunther Kress, London Institute of Education

Introduction

Let me first say that I take it as a particular honour to be asked to give the first in this new series of lectures, to commemorate and honour the work of a man who had a foundational role in the establishment of the enterprise of Applied Linguistics. Given his role, and given that this is the first lecture, it provides an opportunity to assess the distance we have travelled and the directions we have taken; to measure the degree of difference, and the kinds of change in our field; and, to use a currently unfashionable word, to consider what progress we may have made in relation to Pit Corder's foundational work.

I will take his *Introducing Applied Linguistics* as my point of departure. It was first published in 1973, hence written pretty well twenty years ago; and it is still in print. I will quote some lines from the earlier sections of the book, both to give a sense of how he saw the field at the time, and how he seemed to imagine its future. Perhaps the first point to establish is that Pit Corder saw an absolutely essential relation between applied linguistics and linguistics. In the Preface he says: 'I am enough of a purist to believe that 'Applied Linguistics' presupposes 'linguistics'; that one cannot apply what one does not possess' (1973:9). Applied Linguistics thus depends on the best available linguistic theory; and conversely, applied linguistics can only be as good as the linguistic theories which are available for use.

In Chapter one he spends some time considering three theoretical approaches to language which then dominated the field: An approach which focuses on language and the individual, a psychological approach; an approach which focuses on language, society and man, a sociological approach; and thirdly, an approach which focuses on formal properties of language, an approach which, following Hjelmslev, he calls linguistic linguistics. 'It may seem curious to characterize the third approach to language as 'linguistic', thereby suggesting either

Graddol, D , L. Thompson
and M. Byram (eds) (1993)
Language and Culture, Clevedon:
BAAL and Multilingual Matters

that the other two approaches are not concerned with language or that the term linguistics is being used in a rather special way. And, indeed that is precisely the case. It is used here to refer to the approach to language which has been adopted by the study known as linguistics' (1973:25-6). Later in Chapter five he says, 'There has been a general tendency in recent years for these separate approaches to recognize that what they are all trying to explain is in some sense a unitary phenomenon. Consequently a process of 'bridge-building' has been taking place with the emergence of what can be called 'hybrid' disciplines, part linguistic and part psychological (psycholinguistics) and part linguistics and part sociological (sociolinguistics). Are we to see a new superlinguistic theory, a science of semiotics, 'the science of the life of signs in society', as de Saussure called it, which will include and reconcile all these different approaches to language, or will the previously hard-won autonomy of linguistic linguistics in particular disappear. It is too early to give any answers to these questions' (1973:81-2).

Twenty years on, and at the end of the century which de Saussure inaugurated with his prediction about the new 'science of the life of signs in society', it is appropriate, necessary even, to assess whether we are, then, beyond a linguistics which can offer partial explanations only, and nearer to seeing language as a unitary phenomenon, nearer to that new 'Superlinguistic theory' envisaged by Corder. Can we, now, envisage a linguistics that not only restores the connection of 'man and society', but makes that connection the central one?

I am firmly of the view that we are. More I am certain that there are now a set of factors which make it essential to subject linguistic linguistics to a searching review, and to match it against our practices, concerns, and needs.

Here, then, is my list of such factors, each of them a reason for review and a challenge to linguistic linguistics, put forward here in no particular order.

(1) Multi-cultural is now the condition of all the so-called western technological societies, whether officially acknowledged in terms of public policy or not. It is also the condition of many non-technological, non-western societies. Indeed, given the effect of the transnational and transcultural electronic media, and all the currently used technologies of dissemination, multi-culturalism is a fact of most societies. Multi-culturalism, whether of an ethnic or social base, such as class, for instance, makes it impossible to maintain the myth of unified, homogenous, national languages.

(2) Since the beginning of this century there have been fundamental shifts in the economic, hence in the social structures of western

societies. If in the early 1900s approximately 80% of the working population was employed in manual labour and 20% in white-collar work, that proportion is now completely reversed. By the mid 1980s about 75–80% of the workforce in Britain was employed in white-collar or service industries, and approximately 20% in manual work. There has been a similarly fundamental shift in the participation rates of men and women over the course of the last 80 years.

The shift in the economies of the west to the dominance of the tertiary sector has a profound effect on language. Language has become a major technological resource, whether in control or in management, or in the burgeoning areas of cultural production, such as the plethora of media industries, advertising, public relations, etc. These changing uses of and new demands on language are having effects on language not only in terms of giving certain existing practices and forms – whether grammatical or textual – a different salience or an increased prominence, but also in producing far-reaching shifts in the grammatical and textual resources of the language – whether in extending the syntactic potentials of existing rules and forms, in producing new syntactic forms, or in producing a new range of generic textual forms. I am drawing here particularly on the research and writing of a group of linguists at Lancaster University on enterprise culture, and on the work on language and discoursal change of Norman Fairclough.

(3) New technologies are beginning to show effects on our uses of language, and may be expected to produce fundamental changes. I have no wish to fall into a simple-minded technological determinism; in fact, while I do believe that technologies do have an effect in their own right – whether the wheel, the stylus, moveable type, or the internal combustion engine – I do think that their specific effects are shaped and directed by the structures and practices of the cultures and societies in which they are produced, or in which they are taken up in particular ways. Without giving detailed examples, there are several features of such technologies whose social effects and implications we need to consider:: the increase in machine-human interaction in communication (automated tellers, word processors, electronically distributed information, such as e-mail, fax, etc) which has multiple and diverse effects. For instance in the direction of normalising, normativisation of language on the one hand; on the other hand producing social relations which are paradoxical in terms of the social relations which have led to present modes of language and forms of text: e-mail, as an example, mixes instant communication (hitherto the domain of speech) with absence of the participants (hitherto the domain of writing). The increasing speed in interaction at a distance alone is a factor (eg fax, e-mail) which will shape language in the written mode in the direction of what we now consider speech-like forms. There is, for instance, the normative effects of parsing programmes based on particular kinds of linguistic theories with their implicit or explicit ideological positions, and their attendant descriptive effects. All these will affect our field of enquiry.

(4) Present day political agendas are overtly focusing on language and on linguistic issues. This is an effect of the first three factors: an ideological/ political response, on the one hand, asserting national cultural and linguistic identity against the facts of multi-culturalism; and an equally predictable response reflecting the changing significance of language in relation to economic factors and shifts,

reflecting, albeit in a distorted form, the real demands of an economy based on cultural, service and information industries. However badly understood these questions may be by those who formulate them – politicians, captains of industry – they are real enough to call for a theoretical response.

(5) Simultaneously there has been an increasing awareness of the effects of power through and in language on the possibilities for equitable participation in social and cultural life. One can cite here the work done, for instance, on issues such as gender and language, class and language. Linguistics cannot afford to maintain a spurious position of 'objectivity'.

(6) It seems evident that we are in a period which is witnessing a significant shift in the relative valuations, as well as the quantitative load, of the various semiotic modes through which a society produces and reproduces its meanings. In particular, in the domain of public communication there is a noticeable shift from verbal to visual forms of representation and communication. On the one hand this reflects the necessity for new strategies for the maintenance of social control and cohesion, and on the other hand, this has effects on the importance, the 'salience' of language as the public mode of communication, and hence on the functions which language serves in society.

(7) In some theoretical work there is, in parallel, an increasing awareness that language is one, just one, of the number of semiotic modes involved in the production, communication, and change in the meanings and meaning-system of a society. In part this is a response to critiques centred on the 'logocentrism' of dominant social groups or of whole cultures, and associated forms of rationality, which have unequal effects in social structures. In part it is a response to a new and enlarged scope of semiotics as an enterprise, particularly in the form of social semiotics. In these new enquiries it is not even clear at the moment just how one is to value or place language in the total system of semiotic modes.

(8) There has, over the last 10 or 15 years, been an astonishing convergence of work from many directions – from sociology, anthropology, media and cultural studies, from different forms of feminism, linguistics, discourse and conversation analysis, critical discourse analysis, communication studies – onto questions precisely around the connections of language and culture and language and society – the restoration, in Corder's words, of the links of 'man and society'.

(9) Last, but by no means least, there remains for Applied Linguistics, as for a science of language in general, Pit Corder's unanswered question: 'Are we to see a new superlinguistic theory, a science of semiotics, "the science of the life of signs in society", as de Saussure called it, which will include and reconcile all these different approaches to language' (1973:82). Will, what Corder called 'the present unstable constellation of disciplines concerned with language' emerge as a new, productive entity?

In this context, with these pressures, what is our response to Corder's characterization, made in the very early 1970s, and to his speculation about the future? In many ways the situation seems no different: fragmentation and specializations have, if anything, increased. There are now branches of the study of language which either did not exist at all in 1970, or were far less significant then. But that would be to take at face value what might be the discipline's own public account. The reality is different. It shows on the one hand enormous convergence of diverse theoretical work in application, and, on the other, a fundamental shift in the weight or salience of various kinds of work.

In very many ways, it is here, in our work in Applied Linguistics, that a new theory of language is being produced. It is the pressure of application, of dealing with specific, intractable problems, across a wide area of language use, which is producing this shift in focus, a shift in emphasis from the formalistic, autonomous conception of language, to a view of language as a product of cultural and social factors; and hence plausibly explicable only within such a framework. If that is indeed so, it is because the existing theory will not do. In Corder's words 'one cannot apply what one does not possess'.

The answer, then, must be: 'let us make what we need'. Strategically it is important to articulate some of the shortcomings and problems with existing theories, in order to clear the ground, and make the task of constructing the new theory more feasible.

This will be my first move. I will try to illustrate my points by reference to textual examples, and at times suggest possible 'new' alternative theoretical accounts. Before I do I need to stress that I will be offering a critique of Pit Corder's linguistic linguistics', and *not* a critique of the kind of work on language which is now so prominent, and so prominently represented here.

My second move will be to present in a brief summary form the points which emerge from this, as a skeletal outline of the characteristics of the new 'superlinguistics'.

A social linguistics

First then: linguistic linguistics is an a-social theory of language. Given this, it is a theory founded on a monologic rather than a dialogic view of language, and one that takes monoglossia rather than heteroglossia as its starting point. Necessarily, this produces normative theories and makes it into a normative discipline: whether it does so via the social categories of *convention*, or *appropriateness*, or *institution*, or does so via psychologically orientated explanations based on notions of mental structures, cognitive schemata, etc. I should perhaps make it quite plain that for me a social theory of language is not one that sets up an opposition between the psychological and the social. Quite plainly, most of the questions presently dealt with in psycholinguistics, or in cognitive linguistics, or in Applied Linguistics, need to be dealt with in any account of language – but seen as culturally and socially produced. Other aspects will have to become or remain the domain of those disciplines dealing with material/physiological aspects of the brain, of cognition in the broadcast sense. These matters are highly relevant to an understanding of language, in the same way that they are highly relevant to all other forms of human action and practice.

As an a-social theory, linguistic linguistics presently can offer no account of heteroglossia as the normal state of affairs, and of dialogism as the normal form of linguistic practice. This makes impossible any revealing account of the production of text. Take as an example Text 1, a fax sent during the course of the 'Gulf War', from a BBC correspondent to various media organizations around the world, among them RN-SYD Radio National, in Sydney (part of the Australian Broadcasting Commission, the ABC). It is reproduced here in reduced form, with the kinds of smudges typical of this medium, and with some of my own scribblings.

The text in this form, that is, the fax including my scribblings (which preceded a talk I gave for the ABC), records the many voices which participated in its production. There is the writer, Alward; the sub-editor, Howard; the 'talent' – Galwraith; a 'US squadron commander'; the 'allied forces'; and my own 'writing'. Each of these represents a different institution or different places in an institution: the media, the ABC, the BBC, the journalist, the sub-editor; the military, the allied forces, the squadron commander, the Major; the University, the Professor of Communication. Each speaks from a different social position, with different knowledges, different degrees of authority, different power, different interests. Each uses language in a subtly different though recognizable way. At each point there is dialogue, between 'The Allied Forces' and the BBC journalist, between the squadron commander and the journalist, between the journalist/writer and the sub-editor/rewriter, etc. At each of these points there is therefore both a meeting and contest of different social positions, but also a meeting and contest of different forms of language, producing a dynamic of change. Some of these exchanges are barely represented, or barely recoverable. We assume that there is a history of dialogue between pilots like Major Galwraith and the squadron commander, to establish new

SLUG		TALENT	SUBBED	DATE		COPY	CART	TOTAL	CUM
targets opportunity 2	galwrait	howard	Thu Feb	7 07:25	0:23	.15	0:38	
Dest: NOSE		NR:	Writer:alward		Lines: 23				
History:									

EX-RN-SYD

TARGETS opportunity

bbc alward

The allied forces say the bombing of Iraq and Kuwait is now in a
new phase.

Initially the emphasis was on specific targets... such as bridges
and oil installations.

Now a US squadron commander has spoken of attacks against what he
describes as targets of opportunity -- or, as he put it --
taking out...anything that moves.

One of the squadron's pilots -- Major Thomas Galwraith --
describes the change in emphasis.

CART:

BEGINS: WE PRETTY MUCH GO OUT THERE WE WORK A CERTAIN AREA AH AT
NIGHT AND WE PROESCUTE ANY OF THE TARGETS THAT WE MIGHT WITHIN THAT
AREA WE ATTACK THE TARGETS WE OBSERVE ON THE GROUND TARGETS OF
OPPORTUNITY , MOVERS.

ENDS:...

[handwritten annotations]

Text 1: The Gulf War Fax

criteria for bombing missions. The exchange between the ABC journalist who contacted me, and myself, is visible only in my doodlings – and it led to a new text, my radio talk, in which this preceding text was barely 'visible'.

Without a dialogic and heteroglossic view of language, we have no way of accounting for the production of this text. We would be reduced to a description which can provide a list of linguistic features, but with no explanation. For instance, how do we account for the variety of lexical items of 'uttering' – write, sub-edit, say, speak, describe, put it – which occur here, and their meanings in this text. How can we account for the action of one of these participants, the writer, who had produced a text out of this multiplicity of voices to record, I assume, a particular moment in the history of English, namely the specific uses of *work, prosecute,* and in particular, the production of two new word, *targets of opportunity,* and *movers.*

Without a social theory of language, without the categories of heteroglossia and dialogism, we are reduced to a formalistic description, revealing little and nothing. *With* these categories we have an account that provides insight into history, including this small piece of linguistic history, into change, change in relation to various kinds of powers of individuals and institutions. It demonstrates the importance of *text* as one medium, site and record of social interactions, contests and (more or less temporary) resolutions, and their effect on language. Language, in such an approach is seen as one social practice, – one of many -; distinct in its effects and potencies, for instance, as the social practice which documents, summarizes and more or less temporarily or permanently 'fixes' particular histories, states and outcomes in the complex of social forces. As such, language is both effectively involved in the production and reproduction of other social practices; and is itself produced and reproduced by linguistic as well as other social practices and categories.

An historical linguistics

Linguistic linguistics remains an a-historical enterprise, focused on structure or system rather than on the production or change of the systems or the structures. In as far as there is a dynamic aspect – as in certain forms of generative grammars, in systemic functional grammar, or in others – it is a dynamic without history. This rules out any account *either* of the palpable facts of linguistic changes, divergences, and histories, *or* an account of the social production of the complex of systems of language. These questions, which should be at the very centre of any plausible linguistic theory, remain intractable and become either excluded, or exported to marginal areas such as sociolinguistics, pragmatics, historical linguistics, stylistics, etc, the officially designated dumps of problems generated in linguistic theory.

To take as an example the production of the new lexical item *movers* from the text just discussed. Even in this brief text we can see the rudimentary traces of the history of the production of this word, including the last transformational stages from *anything that moves* to *movers*. In most currently available theories there is no possibility of a social and historical account of the production of this item, and so recourse has to be had to notions such as 'coinage', or nominalisation' – both explanations which mystify in different way. Similarly with the quite new textual/generic form of this fax: a new form which has technological, specific social, and historical origins.

Or consider, another instance of linguistic change, though this time not the production of a new word and its addition into the lexico-syntactic system, but the remaking of an existing item, the verb *invade* and its transitivity potential.

> In Central Australia ... the Pitjantjatjara were driven by drought to expand into the territory of a neighbour. Several of these invasions might be partly explained by a domino theory: the coastal invasion of the whites initially pushing over one black domino which in turn pushed down outer dominoes. But it would be sensible to believe that dominoes were also rising and falling occasionally during the centuries of black history. We should be wary of whitewashing the white invasions. We should also be wary of the idea that Australia know of no black invasions.

> Even when Aboriginal tribes clung to their traditional territory, fatal fighting within the same tribe or between members of hostile tribes was common. It is possible that many tribes suffered more deaths through tribal fighting than through warfare with the British colonists in the 19th century (Geoffrey Blainey,1973, *A Land Half Won*)

The social/historical context of this snippet of text is broadly as follows: until the late 1960s, the arrival of whites in Australia and their subsequent history on the continent had been spoken of as 'the settlement of Australia'; a peaceful, uncontested process, in the context where the continent had officially been declared a 'terra nullis', an empty land. By the late 1960s this formulation had ceased to be tenable, in the face of growing evidence of the

widespread extermination of the black population, frequently
with considerable resistance by them. In that context *invasion*
became a politically progressive means of talking about this
history, signalling a number of essential factors: the existence of
an indigenous population, their claim to the land, an
acknowledgement of their resistance, and an indication of the use
of violence and power in the process.

Geoffrey Blainey's use of the term *invasion* therefore marks
him as a politically progressive historian. However, his
grammatical use of the term shows a fundamental tension
between this directly declared position, and other, divergent
elements in his account. The term *invasion* is first given a gloss as
a natural phenomenon ' ... the Pitjantjatjara were driven by
drought to expand into the territory of a neighbour'. *Drought* is
the causative subject/agent of the main clause; the verb *expand* in
the embedded clause is non-causative and non-transitive ('they
expanded into the territory'), and a diffuse, non-directed action.
Blainey's gloss acts as a metaphor for the process of invasion
which, crucially, provides a number of the terms which are
essential in Blainey's remaking of the transitivity potential of
invade: *invasion* as a natural, or naturally caused, process; a non-
causative syntax; a diffuse effect of the action. Textually, the link
between this gloss and the lexical item *invasion* is made by the
anaphoric pronoun *these* 'Several of these invasions ...' The first
use of *invasion* in a linguistically innovatory (and a politically
suitable) sense is the *coastal invasion of the whites*. This
nominalisation is a derived from a historically prior (whether
actually uttered or not). *The whites invade(d) the coast,* (with a
transformational history something like *the coast was invaded by
the whites, the coastal invasion by the whites,* and finally
weakening the causally explicit *by* to the causally less explicit *of,*
which opens the possibility of a reading which has the *whites*
being invaded). The change to the syntactic potential of *invade*
arises from the extension made to the range of objects which
invade may now take. Whereas before *invade* might have been
expected by most readers to need as an object a noun which is a
political entity, a state or nation, here *invade* has as its syntactic
object a noun which denotes a geographic feature, a or the *coast*.
This changes the syntactic potential of the verb in quite
fundamental ways, syntactically and ideologically. political action
carried out with force can now been seen to act on non-political,
merely geographical features. This alters not only the transitivity
potential of *invade*, but its lexical characteristics. Politically there
is an entire difference between invading a state, and invading a

coast. Ideologically, while *settlement* told one kind of lie ('the empty continent'), *invading a coast* tells another (an action emptied of political force affecting a geographical feature). What the progressive historian has reluctantly given with on hand, he has amply recovered with the other.

My point is that here we have a micro-episode in the history of the verb *invade*, and hence in the history of the English language. This history is produced in specific political/social contexts, and it is the characteristics of this context which shape the history of the language. Of course, this *is* a micro-episode, and just one bit of micro-history. Nevertheless, Geoffrey Blainey's history was read for a decade or more by politically progressive Australians, black and white, as a progressive history, and the term *invasion* is still the currently correct term. Given the power of the politically and ideologically approved historian, even such a micro-episode must have far-reaching effects. But without a historically based theory of language, which includes necessarily attention to structurings of power, processes such as these have no explanation, and drop from the agenda or theoretical and political concern.

Directly related to the need for a historically based theory is the problem captured in Pit Corder's phrase 'the hard-won autonomy of linguistics'. This hard-won autonomy of disciplines has many motivations and supports. Who benefits from the autonomy of a discipline? Or from the autonomy of a subject-area – 'the autonomy of language'? The answer to this has to go beyond the individual interest of those who benefit from being employed in institutions, departments of linguistics, or history, etc, to groups who benefit from fragmentations, isolation, alienation of other groups from each other, and the isolation of their interests and concerns. Traditionally the struggle for the autonomy of linguistics has been portrayed as a theoretical and methodological necessity: the elimination of extraneous concerns in order to enable a certain regularisation of the data to be achieved.

What is excluded in the concern for autonomy? Whose interests are served? And whose interests are put aside? In the focus on the language system, on the core syntax, phonology, grammar, what is excluded largely is the language user, socially situated. More precisely, what is excluded is the idea of communication as a social and historical event, an event which includes minimally at least a receiver as well as a producer. There is a more or less implicit focus on the producer, as the one who has produced a particular grammatical form – the receiver/reproducer exists merely as a mirror-imaged carbon-copy of the producer. Any notion of fundamental differences of interest, or of power, are thereby completely elided. Linguistically speaking, in this elision of difference, the existence of difference in language becomes a problem, dealt with by excising that problem from the centre of the theory. Variation and difference appear in marginal sub- or satellite- disciplines to which they have been exported: for instance in stylistics, or pragmatics, or in sociolinguistics.

So in relation to my next example, for instance, the difference in language at the syntactic level would be accounted for as a stylistic variation – where variation means 'variation from a taken for granted norm'

Full Bench announces decision on BLF today

By MATHEW MOORE,
Industrial Reporter

MELBOURNE: A full Bench of the Arbitration Commission will today bring down its decision in the deregistration case against the Builders' Labourers' Federation.

The three-member Bench, headed by Justice Terry Ludeke, will hand down its decision at 10am, just two weeks after it finished hearing evidence in the case, which began seven months ago.

It is considered almost certain that the decision will grant the Federal Government its application, enabling it to deregister the union federally.

A large police contingent is certain to be on hand in case of any demonstration by BLF members, although the union's general secretary, Mr Norman Gallagher, said no security would be necessary as no demonstration was planned.

"They're too busy working and getting the

3.8 [per cent]", he said, maintaining his claim that the BLF members have not been disadvantaged by the commission's refusal to pass on last November's national wage increase.

Mr Gallagher said no officials would be present although the BLF's legal advisers would attend.

"Why should I go?" he said. "I've got work to do. I have had these decisions before. The thing has been going on longer than *Blue Hills*."

If the Federal Government gets its decision as expected, it will then be able to cancel the union's Federal registration, which will trigger Victorian legislation cancelling the registration in Mr Gallagher's home State.

The BLF has already been deregistered as a State organisation in NSW.

Until the Federal Government acts, the BLF will remain a registered body and the complicated business of trying to carve up the union and distribute its members to other unions will not get under way.

The Victorian Government has already released a draft plan for breaking up the union and it is believed the Federal Government has virtually finalised its own actions.

Too busy for court, says Norm

NORM Gallagher will not attend an Arbitration Commission sitting today to hear its decision in the deregistration case against his union.

"I've got work to do" the general secretary of the Builders' Labourers' Federation said last night.

Nor will BLF members demonstrate opposition to the proceedings.

Mr Gallagher said: "They're too busy working and getting the 3.8 (per cent national pay rise)."

He maintained his claim that BLF members were not disadvantaged by the commission's refusal to pass on last November's national wage increase.

Mr Gallagher said he did not know whether the commission would declare, as the Federal Government wants, that his union breached its undertakings and commitments to the national wage-fixing principles.

He said this would lead to a chain of events which would mean deregistration and ultimate dismantling of the union.

Text 3 (above) from Daily Telegraph, Sidney; 4/4/86

Text 2 (left) from Sydney Morning Herald 4/4/86

What is the norm in relation to which one or other or both of them are stylistic variations? Each of these two texts has been produced from a common source, an AAP Wire report. Each has been rewritten to make it linguistically and textually suitable for a specific audience; and therefore is conditioned by factors of the audience for whom it is written. For each of these two audiences each respective text is not at all a stylistic variant, but is precisely the kind of text and syntax which reflects, and accords with the social and cultural world of the reader who is a regular buyer/reader of either newspaper.

It is only when we introduce the notion of communication into linguistic theory, and with it the appearance of the reader as the quality significant participant in the production of the text – never mind its *re*production – that these two texts can be given satisfactory linguistic description, within the centre of this linguistic theory. The writer of the *SMH* report envisages an audience of readers who, in social/political terms, see events of the kind dealt with here in terms of larger institutional structures, abstract relations between institutions of the state – the judiciary, unions, legislation, state governments, etc. The syntactic form of the language which realizes such an attitude and perception is precisely the nominalising syntax, the reduction of process to spatial relations, the reduction of the variety of real actions to a small inventory of lexical items. Textually this is the language which is foregrounded in the SMH: it is not that it doesn't report Norm Gallagher's words (or the reported form of his words), but that they follow, are subordinated to, are embedded in the formal language. In the *Daily Telegraph* by contrast the reportedly spoken words of the union boss are foregrounded, it is they which frame the institutional/formal language to the extent that it appears in this report.

How do we decide which is the stylistic variant, and of what is it a variant? Yet if we adopt, as I would, the theory implicit in my model, we see that the hitherto accepted model of the autonomous, homogeneous language-system, with its core of syntax and phonology, can no longer be sustained. What we have instead are sets of linguistic resources deployed in line with particular social configurations to produce texts which realize these social structures, processes and relations. Individuals experience these texts in their social occasions of production and from that experience build up particular representations of what 'their' language is.This is not a comfortable view and has effects right at the level of syntax. Let me explain by means of yet another example.

Individual readers' experience of texts

School banishes boy too poor to pay for uniform
By Ian MacGregor, Education Correspondent

A Schoolboy was taught in a class on his own because his parents could not afford a uniform, it was revealed yesterday.

The 13-year-old was separated from classmates for several weeks, a community advice organization said. His misery only ended when friends found enough jumble in an Oxfam shop to make a make-shift uniform.

'It is the worst case of this kind we have seen' said Nichola Simpson, head of policy at the National Association of Citizens Advice Bureaux.

'It was very distressing for a boy so young. And he missed out educationally. Children should not suffer like that, especially because they cannot afford a uniform. It was a very hard-hearted thing to do'

Text 4 *Daily Express* 3/5/91

Consider the sentence 'A schoolboy was taught in a class on his own because he could not afford a uniform, it was revealed yesterday'. I am interested in the clause '.... he could not afford a uniform'. What is the grammatical description of the verb *afford*? Some readers treat *afford* as a transitive verb, so that *a uniform* is the direct object, and, in that reading *he* is the agentive subject. Syntactically the analogy is a clause such as *he could not buy a uniform*. Other readers treat *afford* as an intransitive verb, so that *a uniform* is, despite its surface appearance, an indirect object; and *he* cannot be seen as an *agentive* subject. Syntactically the analogy is with a clause such as *he cannot get used to the uniform*, or, *he is unable to have a uniform*. Of course, the distinction of transitive/intransitive is exceedingly crude, and finer, semantically oriented categories would reveal subtler distinctions, though they would simply complicate the picture. In a systemic-functional analysis for instance, we would need to settle whether the example is a material process clause, or a behavioural clause, or possibly even a mental process clause. The headline of the article in fact provides one possible analysis *he is too poor to pay for uniform*. My intention is not to give a satisfactory syntactic analysis (hence I do not wish to enter into debates involving syntactic 'tests' possibilities of passives, the fact that *afford* appears always with a modal auxiliary, etc); that would draw me precisely into the debate which I think is fundamentally incorrect, namely one which assumes that there is a stable linguistic system, in terms of which the answer must be couched – either settling for a particular specific analysis 'on the weight of the evidence' or settling for calling *afford* a multi-valent or syntactically ambiguous verb, in some way.

My point is fundamentally different: namely that different readerships will assign different but for them specific descriptions to this verb. For any one reader therefore *afford* is not multi-valent or ambiguous; and the particular reading given to the verb by that reader derives from a particular social location. Readers who say 'of course they can afford it, I did', 'I had to, they just don't want to' are likely to give the 'transitive reading'. Those readers who say 'How could they be expected to, on income support!?' are likely to give the 'intransitive reading'. It is not difficult to see the underlying difference in social/ideological position.

To restate: a concept of language an autonomous system, and of linguistics as an autonomous discipline, brings with it fundamental political, ideological, theoretical assumptions which in my view are both counter-factual, and more relevantly, in the context of the question of an adequate theory for the tasks of applied linguistics in its many forms, entirely unproductive.

Related to the a-historical and a-social constitution of linguistic theories at the moment, and necessarily a part of that theoretical disposition, is the fact that linguistics had no account of the individual language user as a socially and culturally formed subject. A language user does not come to language as an unformed, culturally or socially vacuous individual, but comes with a complex history of particular experiences of language-as-text, a particular social history, and a particular linguistic history. We do not assume, even in commonsense understandings, that all members of society are the same; so it seems odd that the theoretical linguistic commonsense continues to be that all language users have access in the same way to the same language system, and make use of that system freely and equally for their purposes.

Of course, in many specific applications of linguistics that common-sense had been replaced by an understanding of the socially located character of language use: whether in English for academic purposes, EAP; or in English for special purposes, ESP; the focus is clearly on one socially situated language activity, and on a clear realization that particular aspects of the language system are brought into play, namely precisely those which the social characteristics of that purpose demand.

If we take this as a model for *all* language-use we will come to see that individuals as social subjects participate in a number of such occasions, each with its social and linguistic organization.

Any individual's experience – and subjective make-up – is therefore a complex, formed out of those experiences – not in entirely predictable ways, but certainly also not in merely 'individual' ways. The 'ESP' of any one speaker is a record and result of the speaker's social and linguistic history. It will vary, necessarily, from speaker to speaker, in ways which are accountable to a significant extent, and which, more importantly, provide the language-user with a particular set of linguistic resources. These are the resources which he or she will necessarily use in linguistic interactions. Consequently, whether in spoken interactions, or indeed in the making of a seemingly single-authored (written) text, language users bring different sets of resources into a dynamic interaction, and it is this dynamic of interaction of partially different linguistic resources which is one major cause of linguistic change.

In such as view individual linguistic subjects are the makers of language, agentive in linguistic processes, and in the production of new signs (whether these are syntactical or lexical or textual), and therefore of linguistic change in a direction which is a function of the sum total of resources brought into interactions in particular configurations of power.

So if our ESP or EAP text is a history-text, or a geography-text, we know that we will not merely be teaching history and 'the language of history' but we are involved in a process of producing a particular social and linguistic subject. Such an approach allows us to move beyond, for instance, thinking about textbooks in terms of 'simplification' – that is, producing subject-matter of 'language appropriate for an X-year old child'. In the two brief examples of history-texts below (written for upper primary schools) this approach raises questions about both history *and* language which go beyond structure *and* function, to question effects: why are there so many relational clauses? What is their function in this version of history? What social effect are they likely to have for the reader? What is the function of the agentless passives? What effect will they produce for the reader? etc, etc: both, what kind of historian, and what kind of language user, is projected by this text, and envisaged by its writer?

THE LITTLE GENERAL

Paris, 1804. A little, fat soldier makes himself emperor. The troops and people cheer.

He is NAPOLEON BONAPARTE. Born in the island of Corsica, he started training as a soldier when he was ten years old, and was an officer by the age of sixteen. Ten years later,he was a general, and was soon leading his armies into Austria, Italy and Africa. He built an empire for France.

Napoleon is a superb general. His people and his troops love him. It looks as if nothing can stop him.

But later his armies will be crushed in the Russian snows and the Spanish mountains. His ships will be beaten by the British at TRAFALGAR.

In the end, he will be sent to die on the lonely island of St Helena.

THE SS *GREAT BRITAIN*

Bristol, 1843. A new kind of ship is being launched.

Her name is the *Great Britain*. She is made of iron, not timber. She is kept afloat by air inside the hull.

She is driven by STEAM POWER, but has SAILS to help her when the wind is right. She is the first big ship to be driven by a PROPELLER — it is just under the water at the end of the ship.

In 1845 the *Great Britain* crossed the Atlantic. A year later she was grounded for a whole winter off the Irish coast, but survived the storms and gales of the Atlantic Ocean.

Text 6 (above) 'The SS Great Britain'

Text 5 (left) 'The Little General'.

In the absence of any of these concerns linguistics necessarily remains a gendered discipline (as it remains a discipline impervious to questions raised by other social categories, these simply cannot appear). It might be objected that this is not a question so much of a gendered than of an a-gendered discipline, indifferent to questions of gender, etc. In the sketch of an alternative theory I've given so far *linguistic resources are the product of the interactions of socially formed and situated language-users acting in structures of power*, consequently linguistic form and the multiple and complex systems of resources bear the traces of the action of greater power. The language of a society which has been characterized by structures of institutionalised differences of power along lines of class and gender, among others, is necessarily gendered, and 'classed'. To ignore this history and its effects is to leave language and linguistic theorizing in the domain of past and still existing power distributions, *and* as one of its potent supports.

A historical, social-contextual linguistic theory must have the text as its central unit of analysis and description. Despite at least two decades of work in various forms of Discourse Analysis, Textlinguistics, Conversation Analysis, linguistic linguistics remains sentence or clause-based. Work on *text* is seen as explaining phenomena *beyond, outside* the sentence, hence beyond or outside the domain of linguistics. At the moment here is

either a disjunction of theoretical and descriptive concerns
between clause or sentence level grammars and the various forms
of discourse analysis, or else text is explained in terms of the
'lower' level constituents of clause or sentence. Most approaches
have elements of both. At the moment text-linguistic work is not
seen a shaving an effect on linguistic theorizing about grammars,
thought the converse is certainly the case. Nor is an
understanding of larger textual structures at the moment seen to
have any bearing on the understanding of the constitution of
sentence or below sentence units.

So, at the moment it is entirely usual to think of text as 'made-
up' – in more or less sophisticated versions of 'made-up' – of
clause – and sentence-level units, and to see the structuring of
texts as more or less analogous to the structuring of sentences and
clauses, to see text produced out of sentence-grammar. A
revolutionary, and in my view, necessary, step is to think of the
units of grammar – sentences, clauses, lexis – as being formed in
the production of texts. Certainly, as I argued in *Learning to
Write*, the sentence is much plausibly explained as a *textually* than
a *syntactically* motivated unit. And changes to syntax, as I argued
above, have to be explained from a social/textual point of view.

A linguistic theory appropriate for the range of tasks envisaged
by the concerns of contemporary applied linguistics will need to
take the text and the resources of textual production as the
starting point of theory and of description, together with social
and cultural categories seen as the generative categories of text.
It would have a workable set of categories of text types (genres),
and an account of their production, change, and disappearance.
Lastly it would see linguistic signs at any level derived from,
produced in, and out of, the processes of textual practice,
including the resources of intertextuality.

Linguistics and semiotics

I come now to my final point, namely linguistics as a part of
semiotics. Linguistics remains at this stage a formalistic and not a
semiotic discipline. That is, it has been and remains concerned
with and focused on signifiers (form) rather than signs or better,
focused on the unity of signifier and signified, the forms *and*
meanings of expressions. Consequently, the form-context
dichotomy is as deeply entrenched in linguistic linguistics now as
at any time during this century. It is expressed, among other
things, in the syntax – semantics split in linguistic linguistics, and

in general in the exportation of any concerns with the signified, with matters other than the signifier (form) to clusters of satellite sub-disciplines: pragmatics, semantics, sociolinguistics, discourse analysis, etc. etc. Given that linguistic is not concerned with signs, it cannot deal with 'the life of signs in society'.

The exclusive focus on the signifier has meant that the relation of signifier and signified has not been problematised or theorized in linguistics. Saussure's text has been used to develop a long history and strategy of silence. In linguistics courses there tends to be a ritual reading of a few pages of Saussure's text and a focus on his dictum concerning the arbitrariness of the signifier-signified relation. Of course, an autonomous linguistics needs precisely the theoretical foundation of the arbitrariness of the sign. Its opposite, the assumption of a motivated relation, would lead necessarily to the need for accounts focusing on interaction, communication, social practice, and, with that, loss of autonomy.

Although this is not the place to develop an extended argument around the notion of the motivated relation of signifier and signified, given that I consider it quite central to an appropriate theory of language, I will say just a few words on this here. In a social theory of language, the socially located individual produces signs in particular situations; from particular social positions and therefore, with particular 'interest'. Both of these together provide for her or him sets of criteria which select those aspects of the object to be represented which will be represented (the significant), and they will suggest at the same time the most apt mode of representing what is to be represented, it the signifier. So if a toddler, in looking at a car, finds its wheels the most salient aspect, then if he or she is reproducing it – say in a drawing – he or she will produce a series of circles, and call that 'car'. This produces what is in effect a metaphor: this set of circles is (like) a/this car. When a child climbing a steep slope says 'this is a heavy hill' then the child has abstracted from an event (a relation of action by the child in a physical context) a particular aspect (signified) and has coded that in the best available signifier, the adjective *heavy*. When the writer of the *Sydney Morning Herald* report uses nominalisations, and verbs in an abstracted sense, to report the actions and interactions of institutions, he chooses the apt signifiers (the nominalisations: reifications, and out of time, and the abstractions from real processes) to code what he wishes to signify (the institutional structures and the interrelations and effects). Of course, in this latter case this particular sign – a certain form of writing – already exists, pre-exists the action of the producer of the sign, so the motivation of this sign has a prior history, and this particular reader re-instantiated this history in his remaking of the sign. Or, as a last example, when the historian reworks the existing assign *invasion*, he too does so from a particular 'interest', the troubled relationship between black and white Australians in the late 1960s and early 1970s.

'Interest' varies from social position to social position, from group to group. Hence what is a transparent, motivated relation for the producer is unlikely to be equally transparent for the reader, whose interest may be more or less close or distant from that of the producer. Hence while signs are always motivated in their production, they are never totally transparent in their reception/reading, as the producer's interest is both different to and more or less unknown to the reader.

There is of course also the effect of power. If I am very powerful I can enforce a relation of signifier and signified which, while motivated, is less clearly so for those to whom I am communicating this sign than in other cases where power is not so apparent. Power permits the producer of the sign to act 'wilfully' in the sense that her or his interest is paramount, and the needs of those who are receivers of the sign recede as considerations. Hence power has a distorting effect on the communicative situation – always assuming that we take a situation of equality of power to be the norm in communication. In linguistics as in many other theories this is the assumed normal situation, explicitly or implicitly; both Grice's conversational maxims and Habermas' ideal communication are instances of this. If however we assume, as I do, that all interactions are subject to greater or lesser degrees of power-difference, the situation is not one of 'distortion' but rather, it is the normal condition of communication. One can then establish a hypothesis to the effect that the greater the degree of power-difference between the participants in the interaction, the greater the degree of opacity of the sign (where 'sign' includes all units of the interaction, at all levels). This provides one possible explanation for Saussure's statement: if one is describing a social situation where interactions are marked by great power-difference then one is at the same time describing a situation where signs are marked by great degrees of opacity, and hence it is understandable that signs come to be seen as arbitrary constructs. This account also gives a particular sense to the common saying that 'they speak another language'.

Signs, as social constructs, have histories of smaller and larger scales. However equal the relations of power in the production of a sign initially may have been, and however transparent that sign then was, history, as social actions through time, will inevitably introduce opacity: different groups will have different histories, and hence the recognizable motivation of the sign to the original users will become blurred and perhaps lost to later users. This too will reinforce the notion of the sign as an arbitrary construct.

To sum up this particular argument:

i)   a sign is always the product of a motivated relation between signifier and signified;

ii) it is always the product of a metaphoric process in which the identity – from the producer's point of view – of two elements in the producer's semiotic universe is established;

iii) the point of view is always the effect of particular social and cultural histories and present positioning;

iv) as the producer is a social individual in a particular social place, the production of the sign is always affected by the operations of power;

v)   the operation of power and the effects of history both make the sign more or less transparent or more or less opaque to other users/reproducers of the sign.

Conclusion

I wish, finally, to make one last comment about the present state of linguistic linguistics. Saussure, at the beginning of this century, had seen linguistics as just *one* part of semiology, the general 'science of the life of signs in society'. At the end of this century many critics of culture and social theorists have commented on the logocentric character of Western societies, and the involvement of linguistics in that state of affairs. The point is the same in both cases: language is one, and one only, of many modes of communication. It has so far been the most highly valued and hence the most studies and theorized. But linguistic cannot know either itself or language until the more general 'science of the life of signs of society' can tell us what the other semiotics are like, what their potentials and possibilities are, and what their place in a society's overall communicative assembly is. We will then be better able to understand the real functions of language, its centrality or otherwise to particular functions in society, and its fluctuating history in a particular society. The present period seems to be marked b y an increasing use and significance of the visual semiotic. If that is the case it will inevitably have far-reaching consequences for the place of language (and of its characteristics) in the totality of social and cultural practices. But at the moment this cannot even be a question on the agenda of language theories.

To conclude: it is my firm view that we *have* travelled a long way since Pit Corder posed his questions, at the beginning of the 1970s, over twenty years ago. I am certain that by the end of this century we will have produced more than the outlines of a theory adequate to our present tasks. To achieve this we will need, all of us, to bear in mind, in the hurly-burly of our working lives in our various areas, that we do now have the theoretical resources to begin the task of constructing a theory of language adequate to our present needs. To Pit Corder's question about the possibility of a theory that will include and reconcile all the different approaches to language I am confident we can give a confident answer in the affirmative.

Reference

S. Pit Corder (1973) *Introduction to Applied Linguistics.* Harmondsworth::
    Penguin

Culture is a Verb: Anthropological aspects of language and cultural process

Brian V. Street, University of Sussex

Introduction

My aim is to problematise the concept of 'culture', particularly in a context where it has been linked with language. I will begin by trying to explain my title: I feel a certain temerity as an anthropologist in using such a technical term as 'verb' when addressing a gathering of linguists. My main intention is to signal, from the perspective of recent work in my own discipline, the importance of treating the term 'culture' as signifying process – the active construction of meaning – rather than the somewhat static and reified or nominalising senses in which culture used to be employed in the discipline of anthropology, is sometimes still used in some linguistic circles and has come to be used in everyday 'commonsense' language. However, as I am in the company of linguists, I will attempt to justify the phrase 'culture is a verb' by some appeal to the linguistic literature, notably Halliday's notion of 'grammatical metaphor'. I will begin with a recent application of Halliday's ideas by J. Martin in a paper entitled 'Life as a Noun' that was passed on to me by Mike Stubbs when he saw my title. I will then revert to more familiar territory in citing some of the history and debates in anthropology around the term 'culture', with particular reference to anthropologists such as Talal Asad, David Parkin and Maurice Bloch who have taken an interest in the study of language.

Anthropologists are currently acutely self-conscious in their use of the term culture, worrying about its neo-colonial, racist and nationalist overtones. Rejecting the notion of a fixed inheritance of shared meanings, they prefer, as Robert Thornton argues, to ask not 'what culture is' but 'what culture does' (1988:26). I will attempt to illustrate the practical consequences of these academic debates with reference to discussions of language policy in S. Africa, which I visited recently and where the political implications of the debate around culture arise in especially acute

Graddol, D., L. Thompson
and M. Byram (eds) (1993)
Language and Culture, Clevedon:
BAAL and Multilingual Matters

form. Finally, I will conclude by emphasising the problems we face
in attempting to bring together the concepts of language and
culture in both academic and political contexts.

'Culture' is a verb

Martin examines the discourses of history and of science in some
text books used in Australian junior secondary schools (age 12–16)
and illustrates the uses of nominalisation to 'construct both
disciplines as truth'. He refers to Halliday's notion of
'grammatical metaphor' for a theoretical context from which to
examine the ways in which linguistic resources are employed to
hide the ideological and social bases on which the disciplines are
constructed in these schools. In history, for instance,
'nominalisation is strongly associated with realising events as
participants so that logical connections can be realised inside the
clause'. A history text book explains the possible benefits of war
through the linguistic mechanism of abstraction: 'The
enlargement of Australia's steel-making capacity, and of
chemicals, rubber, metal goods and motor vehicles all owed
something to the demands of war'. Martin deconstructs this
example by 'de-nominalising the participants': 'within this clause
two events are causally related [event 1: 'Australians fought the
war'] *and so* [event 2: 'Australians started making more steel,
chemicals, rubber, metal goods and motor vehicles']. The events,
he argues, are realised nominally rather than verbally whereas in
spoken English the meaning would more likely be constructed as a
clause complex with the events realised verbally'.

> Realising reasoning inside rather than between clauses means
> placing an Agent in a causal relation to its Medium, and this entails
> nominalising events as participants... The enlargement of
> Australia's steel-making capacity and the demands of war are not
> things any more than sound is, but they have to be grammaticalised
> as things in order to reason within the clause.

In science, on the other hand, 'nominalisation is strongly
associated with definitions; its function is to accumulate meanings
so that a technical term can be defined'. The science text book
explains the way in which a tuning fork produces sound through
an identifying clause: 'Sound is a compression wave that can be
heard'. In a similar 'de-nominalisation' of this clause, Martin
points out that 'Sound is not a thing, but has to be dressed up as
one in scientific discourse in order to be defined'.

In both cases the same linguistic resource – nominalisation – is
employed to construct the fields of history and of science and

Martin has to de-nominalise the semiosis to reveal what it disguises: 'The idea that the discourses of science and history are constitutive of those disciplines and negotiable, could not be more hidden'. I would like to argue that a similar de-construction may be necessary with regard to the concept of culture. To borrow Martin's usage 'Culture is not a thing but has to be dressed up as one in social scientific discourse in order to be defined'. To reveal what is hidden here too we need to expose the mechanisms through which culture is nominalised.

There is an interesting analogy here with a critique of traditional definitions of culture within anthropology by Robert Thornton. He argues:

> Part of the problem that besets our current efforts to understand culture is the desire to define it, to say clearly what it is. To define something means to specify its meaning clearly enough so that things which are like it can be clearly distinguished from it. Clear definitions are an essential part of any successful science, or of good speech and clear thought'. (Thornton, 1988:26).

However, the problem is that we tend then to believe the categories and definitions we construct in an essentialist way, as though we had thereby found out what culture is. In fact 'there is not much point in trying to say what culture is... What can be done, however, is to say what culture does'. For what culture does is precisely the work of 'defining words, ideas, things and groups... We all live our lives in terms of definitions, names and categories that culture creates'. The job of studying culture is not of finding and then accepting its definitions but of 'discovering how and what definitions are made, under what circumstances and for what reasons'. These definitions are used, change and sometimes fall into disuse'. Indeed, the very term 'culture' itself, like these other ideas and definitions, changes its meanings and serve different often competing purposes at different times. Culture is an active process of meaning making and contest over definition, including its own definition. This, then, is what I mean by arguing that *Culture is a verb*.

A major critique of British anthropology at the end of the 1970s made a similar point in the context of the role of the study of language in the work of one of the founding ancestors of the discipline in Britain, Malinowski. Talal Asad in the Malinowski lecture 'Anthropology and the Analysis of Ideology' argued that Malinowski's concept of culture is based on a reified notion of 'meaning'. Citing the remarkable range of anthropological texts that use the term 'meaning' in their title, Asad (1979:609) argues that whether they derive from 'the rationalist perspectives of those concerned to assert the universality and priority of cultural classification systems or the empiricist perspectives of those concerned with what they take to be the ultimate datum of flesh-and-bone individuals, interacting intelligently with the real world' this preoccupation with 'meaning' has been a source of much theoretical weakness in the discipline. The major problem has been that the

> basic social object which is presented in the discourse of such anthropologists, whether rationalists or empiricists, is constructed out of an *a priori* system of essential human meanings – an 'authentic culture'.

His critique of this process in one of the classic texts of post-war anthropology – Leach's *Political Systems of Highland Burma* – provides an exemplary model for our present attempts to understand cultural processes and the problems to which they are subject.

The starting point of Leach's study was Kachin identity:

> The problem was that the so-called hill peoples of the north-eastern Burma frontier region were rather diverse in their culture, lived in contrasting ecological settings, spoke a number of quite distinct (often mutually unintelligible) dialects, and were organised in local communities which apparently held to very different political principles.

Leach's answer to this problem was

> that Kachin identity was based on a common 'ritual language' that defined the political economic integrity of the Kachins and through which what could and could not be 'correctly' said in the political discourse of the Kachins was determined. The changes and variations apparent in the region can therefore be rationalised as conceptual moments of the 'same' social structure, their 'meaning' is to be understood in terms of an underlying 'grammar of ritual action'.

Asad's critique of this is not simply that it appears to rule out argument and criticism in Kachin society ' as though 'there is only one language which is 'determined by society''; nor that the origins of Kachin reality may reside in economics and politics rather than ritual and language. Rather,

> The difficulty resides in the very notion of a 'grammar' which is at once the principle that defines the anthropologist's object of discourse and also *the* system of concepts which is held to integrate and define Kachin political and economic life as a whole' (1979:616).

Does such a grammar hold for all economic and political conditions and what are the conditions in which it itself might change: are there 'specific political economic conditions which make certain rhetorical forms objectively possible and Authoritative?' In other words, how is change possible in such an account which appears to define a closed system of 'shared meaningful ideas' as though the question of an 'authentic culture' were a matter for anthropological discovery rather than of contested discourses within a particular region. Mary Douglas, another post-war British anthropologist for whom much of the blame for this essentialism is due according to Asad, similarly founds her work on a flawed theory of language and culture: for her the

> system of human meanings, like a given language, has the function of rendering the structure of cultural experience and of political action isomorphic... the cultural and political conditions for doing and for saying things, as well as the meaningful statements and actions produced in these conditions, are neatly fused together. Nothing can be said or done with meaning if it does not fit into an *a priori* system, the 'authentic culture' which defines the essential social being of the people concerned.

Asad's critique of these approaches also provides us with a basis from which to assess many contemporary concepts of culture: firstly there is the problem of change:

> From such a perspective the transformation of social structure is impossible, or impossible to understand, because there is no social object that is specified independently of a system of human meanings.

There is also the question of power: the anthropological tendency to

> accord a critical priority to systems of human meaning... leaves unposed the question of how different forms of discourse come to be materially produced and maintained as authoritative systems.

He concludes in terms that, as we shall see, are now being taken up by anthropologists in the 1990s:

> Instead of taking the production of 'essential meanings' (in the form of authoritative discourse) in given historical societies as the problem to be explained, anthropology takes the existence of essential meanings (in the form of 'authentic discourse') as the basic concept for defining and explaining historical societies' (p.623).

The reification, and naturalisation of 'culture' hides the kinds of questions about power and social change that are currently at the forefront of anthropological enquiry: ideas and misconceptions drawn from the study of language have had no little influence on this flawed heritage, notably the metaphor of grammar for interpreting social systems and the unselfconscious nominalisation of culture that hides its essentially changing character and process nature.

I will exemplify this argument through a brief summary of a well-known debate in anthropology regarding the nature and role of language in political processes. Maurice Bloch in an introduction to his edited volume *Political Language and Oratory in Traditional Society*, (1975) complained that in their accounts of political processes anthropologists had not paid much attention to actual language, even though a great deal of politics involves 'people speaking to each other'. That volume was intended to redress the balance and Bloch's introduction aimed to set the theoretical framework for analysis of such empirical language events. Bloch looks for 'politics' in features of everyday life and interaction, defining politics more broadly than many of his colleagues who, he argues, had focused simply on the exercise of authority in overt political institutions. Using his own fieldwork amongst the Merina of Madagascar, he suggests that everyday speech and politeness patterns and certain contexts of more formal oratory, are key sites of political transaction. Merina Elders, he maintains, may exercise power by addressing listeners in a speech style that requires limited formal responses and rules out disagreement or criticism. The disallowing of alternatives is achieved pragmatically through the formal characteristics of the discourse they initiate. Bloch constructs an ideal type of this 'formalisation': whereas in everyday speech acts there is a choice of loudness, intonation, syntactic forms, vocabulary, sequence and illustrative material, in 'formalised speech acts' there are fixed loudness patterns, extremely limited choice of intonation, exclusion of some syntactic forms, fixity of sequencing and limitations of illustration (eg. from certain traditional sources, proverbs, scriptures etc.). (Bloch, 1975:13). Whilst the degree of formalisation may vary, so that the two types of speech act represent a continuum rather than a dichotomy, as a heuristic this model is intended to demonstrate how formalisation of language may become a form of power or coercion. Communication is restricted, indeed impoverished, in the sense that the 'fantastic creativity potential of natural language' in which a single utterance can be followed by a whole range of possible responses and language options, is lost. The formalisation of language thus empties it of meaning and of communication potential and prescribes a predicted sequence of utterance and response:

> if the utterance of a speaker predicts what sort of things he will say, it also predicts the answer of the other person as long as this person is accepting the code (1975:19).

It is in this sense that 'the formalisation of language is a way whereby one speaker can coerce the response of another' and is therefore a 'form of social control' (1975:20). It is the illocutionary force of such utterance rather than its propositional meaning that

gives it this power and it is this level of linguistic interaction and
indeed coercion that anthropologists interested in politics ought
to be addressing.

The link between formalisation of language and the
construction of culture can be traced through a number of political
contexts in which a particular social group commandeers the
language as a means of asserting unity under their authority. For
instance,

> the requirement to liken specific events and actions in the present
> to certain fixed events in the past, through reference to certain
> stories and cultural heroes, reduces the ability of language to
> communicate messages concerning specific events, and its ability to
> convey messages leading to particular action... The individuality
> and historicity of events disappear since irrespective of minor
> differences these events are all *like* the scriptural examples'
> (1975:15).

This leads to 'Unity of all under the aegis of accepted values',
says Bloch, a kind of essential meaning that reifies political
processes as fixed cultural norms. The tendency towards unity via
unspecificity means, however, that specific issues cannot
efficiently be tackled since if the formalised oratory is a form of
social control within a fixed set of norms it cannot deal with
individual (hence divisive) innovative action' (1975:16). The
formalisation of language, then, is what serves to construct
culture: it is this which gives apparent fixity, unity and norms to
disparate sets of people on the ground. It is the failure of
anthropologists to recognise this process, perhaps that has led
them to believe in 'culture' as essential meanings in the way that
Asad criticised above. They have accepted the code and have been
as coerced by the language of their informants as have other
powerless listeners to whom such utterances have been
addressed.

This analysis may serve as a means of understanding why
anthropologists have been taken in by a fixed concept of culture. It
does not, however, explain the actions of the actual people being
studied, who might be expected to be more sophisticated in their
recognition of the tricks being pulled on them and have more
strategies for resisting such crude attempts at coercion. David
Parkin in an aptly titled paper 'Political Language' (1984) attacks
Bloch's model of formalised language and the implications he
draws from it for the relationship between language, politics and
culture. The dichotomy between formalised and everyday
language acts is reductionist, he argues: there are not two
languages or codes but a single reality, a dialectic in discourse.
Oratory, for instance, always involves both formalisation and

creativity. Whatever a 'culture' may determine as 'appropriate', speakers assumptions about their audience may differ and different audiences may demand different degrees of formalisation or creativity. The dichotomy should be seen not as an analytic tool with which to compare different cultural practices, but as itself part of the object of study, a strategy available to members themselves.

Some societies, indeed, have words for such a dichotomy, Malagasy for instance distinguishing 'kabary' as formal and predictable speech. This may appear to reinforce Bloch's argument, but Parkin's point is that there is a difference between an analytic account that appears to fix forms of language in relation to forms of authority, and cultural practice in which such claims are part of political contestation and strategy. He concedes:

> It is only fair to say that Bloch was able to capture a critical aspect of traditional oratory, namely the fixed forms by which it was ordinarily defined. But... it is the *idea* of fixity rather than its practice that most typifies oratory amongst most peoples' (1984:351).

Either there is often a *belief* by a people that a form of oratory is formalised and predictable, or we are dealing with the *appearance* say for ceremonial purposes of such oratory'. In practice such forms are not as monolithic or authoritative as Bloch suggests:

> Where there does exist a fixed style, then there is inevitably an alternative oratorical style which allows for more flexible and creative interpretive exchange between speaker and audience. Or else the audience may respond in different ways: repetitive formulae do not necessarily evoke the same responses. Speakers audiences, contexts and the implicit issues constantly change. What an oft-repeated phrase meant on one occasion or at a particular point in the speech need not convey the same meaning later... To remain with the hypothesis that traditional political language stifles creativity and reinforces control comes dangerously close to a tautology: any speech that deviates from this or any audience response which is of a questioning nature, can so easily cause us to assume that the form of oratory is non-traditional, perhaps no more than an innovation' (1984:351)

Parkin cites research on forms of oratory in western societies that supports the more dialectical interpretation of forms of oratory and contrasts the assumption there of the creative capacities of speakers, the skills of persuasion and of exchange with audiences, with the representation of non-European society as somehow more subject to coercion and deception. In fact, all speech making involves some imagining of audience meanings, some brokerage, some attempt not only to persuade but to claim to act on their behalf. He also points out that cultural aspects of language cannot be reduced simply to its performative functions – doing things with words – a tendency in both linguistics and anthropology when the social context of language is addressed. As Pratt states (in 'Anthropology, Language and Linguistics', in Lyons, 1987) attention to the performative functions of language 'should not diminish the attention paid to social context in the analysis of the use of language to make propositions about the world, since this is also fundamentally a social process' (1987:270). Orators, and speakers in general, are making propositions of an epistemological and ontological kind whose impact on an audience cannot be reduced to hortatory rhetoric, formal skills or performative coercion. If we recognise that a western audience may have to be reasoned with and meanings negotiated then, in keeping with anthropological work in other domains, we should extend the same level of analysis to non-European society when we research political language there. Echoing Martin's argument about the power of scientific language to classify, Parkin argues that whilst 'people who retain power to name and objectify others determine the terms of discourse', this process is contestable. Like Asad, he rejects the search for essential meanings and instead wants to study how particular meanings, labels and taxonomies gain their authority. This is not a top-down process of domination but a struggle over discourse:

> within itself, so-called ideological discourse provides creative insights as well as repressive directives... and our problem is how to distinguish these' (1987:360).

Whilst the use of certain relatively fixed terms and phrases may appear in Bloch's sense to 'make up the text of a whole culture or sub-culture', in fact

> such relatively predictable taxonomies do no more than represent the dominant view of the culture. Counterposed to these fixed terms are the more variable expressions which question established assumptions.

The task of anthropology is to provide us with 'micro-historical cases of cultural discourse in action'.

One such example derives from Parkin's own research amongst Luo in Kenya. 'Luo elders speak authoritatively in the firm taxonomy of segmentary lineages, but young men and women seek more modern and also much more variable ways of opposing such tradition'. Young men become elders themselves but women remain subordinate, and so it was predicted that it would have to be the latter who would introduce new vocabulary into the ideological discourses of Luo society. In fact the very possibility of this was facilitated by the way in which the elders fell prey to the belief in rhetorical fixity described by Bloch. Elders constantly harangued women and young men to observe traditional custom. But their own idea of custom and the terms they used to describe it were so fixed that they could not see that the majority of the population by then understood something else by them. 'Under the cover of set terms and vocabulary, the rebellious and disadvantaged had smuggled in new meanings' (1987:352) Parkin, then, puts forward the notion of internal cultural debate, emphasising process and change in cultural as well as political identity, in contrast with Bloch's emphasis on fixity and coercion. Different models of society and of the political generate different ideas about the role of language and cultural process.

The changes in these ideas in recent years, partly as a result of the debates and critiques cited above, have left anthropologists wary about the concept of culture. Robert Thornton in a 1988 paper 'Culture: a contemporary definition' (Boonzaier et al, 1988) suggests that the history of the idea is more significant than its actual value in present-day study. With reference to the South African situation, for instance, he argues that

> it is often the history of ethnological *publications* rather than the real history of South African people, that has had most influence in the shaping of political boundaries... The history of the idea has been deeply bound up with 19th century ideas of 'society', 'nation' and 'organism' all of which have in common the functionalist idea of a self-contained and self-regulating *wholeness*,

a notion that in the S. African context has helped reinforce the idea of 'race' and of separate development. From an academic point of view, a major factor in facilitating the development of this sense of culture has been the observer's lack of reflexivity:

> The fact that the observer must also be part of the social situation that is observed was left out of earlier descriptions of 'cultures'. This created the effect of 'cultures' existing by themselves, the objects of scientific disinterested observation.

Thornton would like to distinguish between singular and plural uses of the concept. In S. Africa the plural uses of the term are politically loaded: 'the concepts of 'different cultures' and 'own' culture have become central to the political thought of most S. Africans' (1988:24). For the most part, these political uses of the word 'culture' are not about culture at all as [he uses] the term here but rather about cultures. In this case, it is the final 's' that makes all the difference' (1988:24). It is the final 's', the plural use of the term, that enables the kind of separation of people on the basis of supposed cultural differences that underpins apartheid.

Thornton, then, would prefer to use the term in the singular: in this sense, he argues, 'culture is best thought of as a resource' and like other resources it does not belong exclusively to any one group or individual.

> while there are differences in the way people behave and think and live, this reflects their differing access to cultural resources, as well as their use of these resources to make statements to each other and about themselves.

One such statement is the assertion of 'identity and group membership'. In the S. African context such claims comprise:

> whole assemblages of safari-suits and tee-shirts, Zulu dance and sakkie-sakkie, Afrikaans, English, gamtaal and slang – together with all of the ways of using and expressing these and many other material and conceptual resources... The claim to 'one's own culture' and the apparent multitude of 'different cultures' in S. Africa are therefore part of the idioms or usages of culture-in-general (1988:23).

But this is a process rather than a state of being: culture *does* rather than *is*. For instance:

> one thing that culture does is create boundaries of class, ethnicity (identification with a larger historical group), race, gender, neighbourhood, generation, and territory within which we all live. Boundaries are created and maintained when people observe, learn and finally internalise the rituals and habits of speech, the disposition and dress of their bodies and modes of thought to the extent that they become entirely automatic and unconscious. These boundaries come to seem uniquely real and permanent. Their creation through cultural means is only obvious when we step outside our normal day-to-day interactions (1988:27).

As with Parkin's critique of Bloch, Thornton warns us not to confuse these everyday or political uses of the term culture 'with an accurate *understanding* of what culture is and what it does'.

> An understanding of culture, then, is not simply a knowledge of differences, but rather an understanding of how and why differences in language, thought, use of materials and behaviours have come about. There are certainly cultural differences, just as there are differences in climate or personality or the various batches of the same colour of paint – but these differences have meanings, functions and histories. Contemporary cultural studies look at these meanings, functions and histories in order to understand the differences; they do not use the apparent 'fact' of differences to explain history, politics and beliefs (1988:25).

Some contemporary anthropologists would go even further than Thornton and reject not only the plural use of the concept 'cultures' but also the singular noun – culture. To label particular groups of people 'a' or 'the' culture – the Xhosa, the British, the Indians – is to create the reification criticised by Asad and Parkin amongst others and which equally underpins the separation of peoples in S. Africa – Zulu, Xhosa, Sisotho etc. During a recent visit to that country I was struck by how powerfully this idea still worked within the education system. Here students are taught in their 'mother tongue' for the first few years of primary school, learning english as a second language at the same time. Then at Standard 3 they switch from English as study to English as medium of instruction, whilst their mother tongue is now taught as study. A major problem with this strategy is the artificiality of the concept of mother tongue. Young children living in urban townships may find themselves living next door to Nguni speakers, across the road from Sesotho, whilst their parents derive variously from Xhosa or other language groups.Their everyday 'first language', then, may be some sort of urban creole, a subject ripe for sociolinguistic research at this moment. Such children when they enter school have a 'mother tongue' designated for them and have to spend three or four years learning through it, even though it may be as alien for them as english. The construction of an idealised 'Zulu' or 'Xhosa' language form is as artificial as the notion of 'a' Zulu or Xhosa culture. As Thornton points out, these are resources in a struggle for goods and for power in modern S. Africa – as in the Zulu claim that spears are a 'cultural weapon' or the contests and disputes over which language children should speak documented by Mukul Saxena in Punjabi communities in London (Saxena, 1991).

The state, in S. Africa through the legal mechanisms of apartheid and in the UK as well as S. Africa still through the education system, has an interest in reifying the linguistic and the cultural resources through which these contests are expressed, as indeed do many of the oppressed themselves. Liberal educationalists coming to S. Africa from the UK, have found themselves confronted with difficult contradictions in this situation: in the UK, authorities such as ILEA developed as part of their anti-racist policies concern for language maintenance and cultural reinforcement; in S. Africa such ideas smack of apartheid and the old bantustan policy. The potential of cultural reification for political division and control is nowhere more evident as is the need for more careful, politically sensitive uses of concepts such as culture. Thornton argues that in reality the identities and differences employed in such a context often

> overlap and conflict with each other. They almost never correspond with other identities in a way that would justify the belief that each 'people' has a uniquely different culture' (1988:27).

The fact that they appear to do so may be as much a product of mistaken academic theorising as it is of virulent political strategies.

The problems with the concept of culture are, then, manifold. Writers have variously criticised the notion of 'a' culture; of 'the' culture; of cultures with an s. They have also challenged the analogy with language that appeared so fruitful in the post-war years; the notion of an underlying 'grammar' of culture has been attacked as has the very attention to language as a model for understanding systems of meaning. The ideas of both culture and of language have been seen as reified, static, and essentialist. Nor are these criticisms restricted to academic debate: fears have been expressed about the use of the concept of culture to reinforce racial and ethnocentric divisions, such as in the system of apartheid; and in the debates about 'multiculturalism' in Europe (which I have not time to enter here) the notion of culture has been seen as deflecting attention away from understanding power relations; the focus on 'saris and samozas' in UK multicultural education, for instance, has been criticised for drawing attention to trivial signs of difference whilst gross political and economic inequalities remain.

What then, if anything, is to be salvaged from a concept that, as Raymond Williams has shown, has a long and complex history in European thought and that appeared in my own discipline anthropology to be the defining focus of a new study of humankind? I will conclude with a consideration of some recent anthropological studies that appear to argue for the continued distinctiveness of the discipline at the same time as rejecting the notion of culture as its focus.

Jane Cowan in *Dance and the Body Politic in Northern Greece* (Princeton, 1990) frames her account of both gender relations and of culture in now familiar terms:

> It is common in anthropological discussions to talk in terms of *the* gender ideas of or within a culture, but such formulation remains problematical. Although what culture is and how it works remain among the most vexed questions within anthropology, the concept of culture retains traces of its functionalist origins. It continues to be understood as the articulation of moral consensus and of shared symbols, beliefs, values, ideas. The problem is *not* that the claims are spurious and that nothing is shared. The problem, rather, is that when culture is defined as that which is shared, questions about this sharedness – is it actually shared? to what extent? By whom? How does it come to be shared? – disappear by definition. The conventions of talking about the gender ideas of the 'X' exaggerate the impression of internal coherence within a society. They can also lead us to search for – and then, in our analysis, to privilege – an 'indigenous' set of gender ideas that is deemed more authentic than

those expressed by others in the same community or in the broader society' (1990:11).

Living in Greece at the time of a new socialist government, when feminist platforms had a very public airing and the 'naturalness' of the traditional order was being questioned, also made Cowan uncomfortable with 'the monolithic implications of such models of culture'.

> Grappling with problems of how best to represent the plural, sometimes querulous, voices I heard raised on the subject of gender, I have found a consensual notion of culture unhelpful (1990:12).

But she does not want to return to an individualistic model: there are patterns and there are social relations that underpin and help explain individual actions and social anthropologists are particularly interested in exposing and exploring these currents. Cowan resolves this dilemma by appealing to Gramsci's concept of 'hegemony', the 'predominance obtained by consent rather than force of one class or group over other classes' (quoted from Femia, 1981:24; Cowan, 1990:12). There are elements of this usage which might appear not unlike aspects of 'culture' criticised above. For instance, Femia sees the 'internal control' exercised by hegemony – in contrast with the external control of the state's repressive apparatuses – as

> an order in which a common social-moral language is spoken, in which one concept of reality is dominant, informing with its spirit all modes of thought and behaviour.

The difference, as writers like Talal Asad within anthropology and Norman Fairclough within linguistics (*Language and Power*, 1989) would argue, is that the notion of hegemony problematises how a common social-moral language – a given discourse – achieves and reproduces its dominance, whereas earlier accounts of culture appeared to accept at face value the representations of the dominant group and their claim to speak for all. As Asad states, we should take

> the production of 'essential meanings' in the form of (authoritative discourse) in given historical societies as the problem to be explained rather than, as in traditional anthropology, taking the existence of essential meanings (in the form of 'authentic discourse') as the basic concept for defining and explaining historical societies (Asad, 1970:623).

It is interesting to see anthropologists like Cowan, writing in 1990, so closely echoing these words of Asad in 1970 in her attempts to make sense of gender ideas in contemporary Europe

There has, however, been some refining of the notion of 'authoritative discourse', to avoid the appearance of a top-down domination of all by a small elite, as though the majority were passive recipients of dominant language and thought. As she points out, Gramsci himself

> did not conceptualise hegemony as a necessarily oppressive process. To the contrary, he saw the development of an alternative hegemony of the working class... an open, expansive and critical hegemony... as essential in the formation of a just society.

Applying this to her own ethnography in the villages of northern Greece, Cowan writes:

> Approaching the processes of gender construction in Sohos in terms of a notion of hegemony entails not a dismissal of 'culture' but a reformulation of it. As Williams writes: 'Hegemony is in the strongest sense a 'culture', but a culture which has also to be seen as the lived dominance and subordination of particular classes' ... The analytic usefulness of the concept of hegemony is that rather than presupposing a moral consensus, it makes it problematical. The concept thus opens up the question of how members of different social groups – variously positioned – accept, manipulate, use or contest hegemonic (that is dominant) ideas. (Cowan, 1990:12)

She is aware that there are elements of this position which seem to have simply reformulated 'culture' back into its old position, but argues that it now carries a different meaning:

> Although the notion of hegemony may appear just as totalising as any concept of culture, it is best understood as a process that always entails the possibility of resistance as well as of accommodation. Hegemony powerfully penetrates individuals' senses and their senses of themselves, yet it is never total or totally determining. ... The concept of hegemony explicitly makes problematical the links between consciousness, sensory experience, and power in a way that the concept of culture, as a set of collectively shared symbols and meanings, does not. (1990:12)

Applying these ideas to gender practices in contemporary Greece, she believes, enables her to maintain the anthropological advantage of seeing the patterns and constraints of social life at the same time as recognising – in a post-modern sense – their multivocal and contradictory character and giving voice to local perceptions and differences She focuses on situations of sociability – social practices such as coffee drinking, celebrating and dancing – and notes that even whilst they connote spontaneity and freedom, they are also 'surprisingly conventionalised'. Indeed, what she found

> especially striking about the bodily and social practices of the contexts of sociability she studies, was the compulsory quality they often have. Because the practices of pleasure and conviviality are also practices of reciprocal social exchange, it is difficult to opt out of them without being seen as arrogant, odd, or unsociable. In any case, opting out is not always an option. When Sohoians (and other

> Greeks) say 'That's how we do it', they admit that they are both enabled and constrained by their social forms – in this instance by their celebratory practices

Cowan see her task as 'to show the ways power, submission, and pleasure come together – or come apart – in the process'. This, then, is what I mean by saying that that contemporary anthropologists see culture as a process: *culture is a verb.*

The emphasis in Cowan's work on bodily movement and on non-linguistic aspects of communications raises a further issue regarding the relationship between language and culture, that was already hinted at in Asad's critique of the 'grammatical' model of culture. Have students of society placed too much emphasis on the role of language in communication, whether as model or as vehicle of cultural process? A recent paper by Maurice Bloch, currently much talked about in anthropological circles, makes this point in a way that claims to challenge still further traditional anthropological conceptualisations of their object of study. In 'Language, anthropology and cognitive science' (Bloch, 1991) he argues that 'anthropology has relied upon a psychologically misleading and overly linguistic model of culture'. Recent work in cognitive science and psychology, he argues shows that 'concepts are principally formed independently of language. Studies of expertise, for instance, 'show that in order to become an expert at a familiar task or set of tasks, a person needs to organise his or her knowledge in a way that is not language-like'. He uses the theory of 'connectionism to suggest that most cultural knowledge cannot therefore be organised in the sentential logical form characteristic of language'. There is, however, still a role for anthropology because

> the traditional anthropological method of participant observation enables the cognitive scientist to understand cultural knowledge without the dangerous intermediary of language' (1991:183).

There has traditionally been a division within anthropology between 'cultural anthropology' and 'social anthropology'.

> Cultural anthropologists study culture. This can be defined as that which needs to be known in order to operate reasonably effectively in a specific human environment.

Social anthropologists, on the other hand, 'traditionally study social organisation and the behaviour by means of which people relate to each other'. The distinction is not absolute, although it has tended to be reinforced by institutional and national divisions: the British tradition, for instance, has emphasised social anthropology and the american tradition cultural anthropology. Cultural anthropologists, however, 'know that they cannot get at culture directly, but only through observation of communicative activity, verbal or otherwise' of the kind indicated by Cowan in her study of 'bodily and social practices of sociability'. Social anthropologists, however, are equally aware that they cannot understand actions and relations

> if they do not construct, probably in imagination, a representation of the culture of the people they study ... Some concept of culture is therefore essential to all social and cultural anthropologies' (1991:184).

Moreover, and of direct relevance to the topic of this conference, Bloch argues that in both anthropologies it has been assumed that

> this notion of culture is inseparably linked to language, on the grounds that culture is thought and transmitted as a text through language, or that culture is ultimately 'language-like', consisting of linked linear propositions.

However, it is precisely these two assumptions about culture and language that Bloch wishes to challenge and which he claims have remained unexamined in the discipline.

> If culture is the whole or a part of what people must know in particular social environments in order to operate efficiently, it follows first that people must have acquired this knowledge, either through the development of innate potentials, or from external sources, or from a combination of both, and secondly that this acquired knowledge is being continually stored in a manner that makes it relatively accessible when necessary (p.184).

These processes of learning and of storage are what cognitive scientists study and they mean that anthropologists' concerns place them right in the middle of the cognitive sciences, although they have seldom been aware of this or attempted to make their theories compatible with what is known from these disciplines.

The aspect of this of interest to us here is Bloch's focus on the 'importance or otherwise of language or language-like phenomena for cultural knowledge'. In particular he is concerned with questions of classificatory concept formation. Anthropologists, he suggests, have traditionally exaggerated the role of cultural variation in this process with their emphasis on the notion of 'cultural models' which have underplayed the universal predispositions out of which specific forms of knowledge emerge. Here, as we have seen, the concept of culture has overstated difference and reified forms of knowledge. Bloch, however, is more interested in those recent theories of concept formation within cognitive science that suggest a looser basis for concept formation: 'concepts are formed through reference back to rather vague and provisional 'prototypes' which anchor loosely formed 'families' of specific instances', in contrast with the old idea that 'the child learns classificatory concepts as minimal and necessary definitions'. The new view assumes that

> the mental form of classificatory concepts, essential building blocks of culture, involves loose and implicit practical-cum-theoretical pattern networks of knowledge.

These 'chunked networks of loose procedures, Bloch suggests, have been likened to scripts' and 'schemata', rather than as in the old view to checklists and dictionary-like entries. The implications of this for the study of language and culture are radical:

> That there is no inevitable connection between concepts and words is shown by the now well-established fact that concepts can and do exist independently of language.

The concept-first theory of thinking (children have the concept 'house' before they can say the word) implies therefore that 'language is not essential for conceptual thought'. In practice the distinction between lexical and mental concepts allows for the notion of a dialectical relation between them, a 'continual back and forth movement between aspects of classification which are introduced through language and mental concepts, as the child learns to express these concepts through words'. Through this process 'originally non-linguistic knowledge is partly transformed as it becomes linguistic'. This linguistic aspect of knowledge is, however, only part of the way in which knowledge is structured and anyone interested in culture has to look beyond this to the varieties of non-linguistic ways in which cultural knowledge is built. Similarly, the ways in which cultural knowledge is transmitted also involves a much larger non-linguistic aspect than generally appreciated by anthropologists. Perhaps their own provenance in schooled societies makes them over-emphasise the significance of explicit instruction: in non-industrialised societies, however,

> most of what takes people's time and energy – including such practices as how to wash both the body and clothes, how to cook, how to cultivate, etc. – are learned very gradually through imitation and tentative participation. (1991:186)

'The cultural specificity, complexity and embeddedness of such tasks, and their character as not linguistically explicit' may have been noted by previous anthropologists but, according to Bloch, 'they have rarely been studied satisfactorily'. Formal craft learning tends to have been studied more, but even here anthropologists have noted with surprise what a small role language plays. Goody, for instance, in her study of weavers in Ghana:

was amazed at the small part played by questioning and speaking in teaching apprentices.

The implications of this may be larger than simply differences in cultural pedagogies:

> it may be that certain kinds of knowledge that underlies performance of complex practical tasks requires that it be non-linguistic.

These arguments have considerable implications for another debate within the area of language and culture with which this Association has been concerned: the significance of the acquisition of literacy for society and for cognitive processes. Where Goody, Olson, Ong and others have argued that literacy is associated with large advances in cognitive processing, and with radical shifts in the nature of society to such an extent that there is a 'great divide' between pre-literate and literate societies, writers in the 'New Literacy Studies', including linguists like Mike Stubbs and anthropologists like myself, have argued that this position is flawed both empirically and theoretically. Ethnographic accounts make it evident that members of societies with little or no literacy can nevertheless perform the complex cognitive processes, achieve the metalinguistic awareness and perform the logical operations that Goody, Ong, Olson and others would attribute to literate society (Cf. Finnegan, 1988). Literacy practices vary with cultural context, there is not a single, monolithic, autonomous literacy, whose consequences for individuals and societies can be read off as a result of its intrinsic characteristics: rather there are 'literacies' whose character and consequences have to be specified for each context. The importance of Bloch's claims above for this argument are that they appear to allow for the possibility that a great deal of complex cognitive processing is taking place irrespective of either literacy or language. The apparatuses for storing and transmitting cultural knowledge specified by 'connectionism', including parallel processing units and networks, non-linguistic mental models, schema and frames appear also to include many of the procedures frequently attributed to literacy, such as lists and tables, ramus devices and possibly the kinds of work with Hypercard being done by another of our colleagues Ulrike Meinhof. In the context of language teaching programmes that also take account of the transmission and storage of cultural knowledge, she is using computer-based software systems such as Hypercard for the 'conscious building of metalinguistic and contextual knowledge' (Meinhof, 1989:15). It may be that the processing units she is calling on are very similar to the devices which Bloch and the cognitive scientists are describing in terms of 'connectionism'. The Malagasy peasant stores and transmits his cultural knowledge, and is able to handle complex cognitive processes through the use of units and systems like this, independently not only of language use in general, as Bloch argues, but also of whether he has been trained specifically in literacy.

This is significant for debates about the 'great divide' in literacy and about the role of literacy in second language learning. As Dubin says in a challenge to autonomous models of literacy and of language teaching, in teaching people to be literate in a second language we are teaching much more than decoding and language skills: we are also imparting often hidden cultural knowledge about what it is to read and write in a given culture, that is to say frames and schema for actually using the specific linguistic knowledge being imparted that may themselves not be operating at a linguistic level (Dubin, 1989:170.)

Conclusion

The storage and transmission of both language and of cultural knowledge, then, appear to involve a number of processes that are not captured by study of language alone. This has considerable implications for our account of language, culture and their relationship. We have already seen that anthropologists are now extremely sceptical of many traditional ways of thinking about and of describing culture. In a context such as this it seems appropriate that they are advising us to be careful of the linguistic ways in which we encode our accounts of culture: to be wary of the usage 'a' culture, or 'the' culture or cultures with an s. Martin's concerns about the role of nominalisation in constructing disciplines, reminded us that similarly 'Culture is not a thing but has to be dressed up as one in social scientific discourse in order to be defined'. We then found social scientists from Asad in 1970 to Cowan in 1990 questioning this discourse and arguing against the reification, fixity and essentialising of 'culture'. At the same time, the ways in which language has been conceptualised in relation to culture has also been problematised. The notion of language as a model for culture, in the sense that a grammar might be written for culture as it has been for language has been rejected by recent anthropologists. Now, not only is language as a model but also language as the vehicle or medium of culture being questioned. Whilst not wishing to deny the significance of language in cultural processes, Bloch and others are now suggesting that anthropologists at least have overstated its role and argue that study of the storage and transmission of cultural knowledge should attend more to what he calls 'non-linguistic' procedures: he would have us study cultural knowledge 'without the dangerous intermediary of language'.

I said at the outset that I wanted to problematise the concept of culture in a context such as this where its links with language are being made explicit. I suspect that I have provided more problems than solutions, but if every time the term 'culture' is uttered warning bells ring and neon lights flash, (i.e. non-linguistic features of our cultural knowledge), then I shall feel I have succeeded.

References

Asad,T (1980)'Anthropology and the Analysis of Ideology', *Man* **14**:607-27

Bell,J (1990) ed. *TESL Talk, vol. 20, no. 1*, Ontario

Bloch,M (1975) ed. *Political Language and Oratory in Traditional Society*, New York:Academic Press

Bloch,M (1991) 'Language, anthropology and cognitive science', *Man*, **26**:183-97

Cowan,J (1990) *Dance and the Body Politic in Northern Greece*, Princeton: Princeton U.P.

Dubin,F (1989) 'Situating Literacy within traditions of communicative competence', *Applied Linguistics*, **10**:171-81.

Fairclough,N (1989) *Language and Power*, London: Longman

Finnegan,R (1988) *Literacy and Orality*, Oxford: Blackwell.

Goody,J (1977) *The Domestication of the Savage Mind*, Cambridge: CUP

Grillo,R, Pratt,J & Street,B (1987) 'Anthropology, Linguistics and Language', in *New Horizons in Linguistics 2*, ed. J. Lyons et al. Harmondsworth: Penguin

Martin,J.R. (1991) 'Life as a Noun: arresting the universe in science and humanities' (unpublished ms)

Meinhof,U (1989) 'Double talk in news broadcasts: a cross-cultural comparison of pictures and texts in television news', paper to BAAL (1989

Parkin,D (1984) 'Political Language', *Annual Review of Anthropology*, **13**:345-65

Street,B (1985) *Literacy in Theory and Practice*, Cambridge: CUP

Street,B (forthcoming) ed. *Cross-Cultural Approaches to Literacy*, Cambridge: CUP

Stubbs,M (1980) *Language and Literacy* London: RKP.

Thornton,R (1988) 'Culture: a contemporary definition', in *Keywords*, ed. E. Boonzaeir & J. Sharp. Cape Town: David Philip.

Discourse and Cultural Change in the Enterprise Culture

Norman Fairclough, Lancaster University

Introduction

The aspect of language and culture I shall discuss is language and cultural change, referring specifically to contemporary Britain, I shall begin by suggesting that language and discourse have an important role in the restructuring of social identities within processes of cultural change. However, linguistics and discourse analysis are not too well equipped to contribute to studies of cultural change, partly because what I will call the 'identity functions' of language and discourse have been relatively neglected. I shall then refer to a study I have published of discursive aspects of cultural change in the enterprise culture, and I shall suggest on the basis of this study ways in which linguistics and discourse analysis need strengthening with regard to identity functions, but then go on to argue that the study is limited in ways which suggest further directions for strengthening discourse analysis in this regard. I shall conclude with the proposal that critical linguistics and critical discourse analysis should be concerned with issues of reconstructing as well as deconstructing social identity in discourse, drawing upon a paper I am writing with Paul Thibault of the University of Bologna.

Language, identity and cultural change

In current studies of social change there is a significant emphasis on changes in culture – in symbolic practices and meanings, cultural value, forms of self and senses of self, etc – which is presumably attributable to increased emphasis on cultural means of social integration and social control in modern societies, identified for instance by Bernstein in a shift towards greater reliance on symbolic modes of control (Bernstein 1991). Issues of social identity, the self, subjectivity are at the heart of studies of cultural change. But cultural change is constituted to a significant

Graddol, D , L. Thompson
and M. Byram (eds) (1993)
Language and Culture, Clevedon:
BAAL and Multilingual Matters

degree in changing discursive practices and within th'
linguistic practices. So the issue of language and dis
construction and reconstruction of social identitie'
one. Potentially, language studies has a great deal tc
research on cultural change. However, this potentia
is limited by a tradition in language studies w.....
marginalised questions of social identity. In much of mainstream
linguistics, questions of identity have entered the picture only in
terms of the concept of 'expression' which presupposes a pre-
linguistic and prediscursive conceptions of the subject, and ignores
the constitutive effects of discourse on social identity. This has
been corrected to some extent in recent discourse analysis, though
often in a one-sided way which emphasizes the social positioning
of subjects at the expense of their action as agents (an issue I
return to).

Attempts to engineer cultural change are a significant
dimension of contemporary cultural change, a feature of what
Giddens for example identifies as the reflexivity of modernity.
Enterprise culture is a case in point. Sell also Hochschild's
important study of the engineered 'emotional labour' of air
hostesses. Cultural engineering also involves engineering of
discursive and linguistic practices. I have discussed aspects of this
in terms of 'synthetic personalisation' in my Language and Power,
the simulation of informal face-to-face talk in institutional
contexts, and in terms of 'technologisation of discourse' in my
1990 paper with that little, the increasing institutionalisation of
research into, design of, and training in discursive practices (as in
the case of air hostesses). Moreover, cultural engineering may as
Hochschild shows have deeply problematical effects on people's
social identities (Giddens would argue that modern life itself
entails such problematisation). The reconstruction of
problematised social identities is therefore an issue, which again
has discursive and linguistic dimensions.

Enterprise culture

I now want to illustrate the relevance of language and discourse
to questions of social identity in cultural change by referring to
some texts associated with the 'enterprise culture'. The emphasis
in this example is upon the engineering of change and attempts to
position subjects – this limits the light it can shed on questions of
discourse and identity as I'll show later.

The enterprise culture as a target for cultural engineering was a brainchild of the Thatcher administration. It started from an emphasis on the economy and markets, but shifted in the 1980s to a project for bringing about cultural and psychological change to make people 'enterprising' (e.g. through the Enterprise in Higher Education initiative). One of its architects was Lord Young, responsible for the Enterprise Unit in the Cabinet Office from 1984, Minister of Employment in 1985, and Secretary of State at the Department of Trade and Industry (which he renamed the Department of Enterprise) in 1987.

In my paper 'What might we mean by enterprise discourse?' I looked at speeches by Lord Young and texts produced by the DTI on the enterprise initiative. The paper argues that the engineering of language is an important part of the engineering of the enterprise culture, and important especially in the engineering of identity – the attempt to construct the 'enterprising self'. The word enterprise itself for example is the focus of extensive semantic engineering: it is constantly being defined and redefined (1-3 in Appendix I are examples), but also used in shifting senses according to political contexts and strategies. The main meanings of enterprise are the meaning of 'business', 'private enterprise', which significantly occurs without the modifier private in these speeches; and the meanings of the word which relate to personal qualities ('being enterprising') and therefore identity, with a scale running from personal qualities specifically related to business (e.g. the ability to exploit a market) to more general personal qualities (e.g. willingness to take responsibility for oneself). These form I suggest a field, a meaning potential and ambivalence potential, upon which successive transformations are effected in accordance with wider strategies – an ambivalence potential in the sense that the unmarked form enterprise can often carry any of these meanings. The process is illustrated in examples 4-10. Notice also that the grammar of transitivity is significant in these examples: what sort of participant enterprise functions as in which process types. The metaphor of field and transformations also carries over to relations between discourses in Young's speeches, realized linguistically in collocational relations between vocabularies; the discourse of enterprise is combined with discourses of skill, consumption etc in shifting configurations, Extracts 7-10 give a sense of this, and show the significance of conjunction. The constructions of the enterprising self in these speeches are disseminated through various interdiscursive channels of distribution into the discursive practices of media, education, management, social services and so on. In the paper, I look briefly at this cultural diffusion in the case of a pamphlet on the enterprise initiative put out by the DTI. The pamphlet consists of double-page spreads each dealing with one of the particular enterprise initiatives – the counselling, marketing, design initiatives for example. I've reproduced the *Design Initiative* in Appendix 2. The initial 'orientation' section of 3 lines beneath the heading occurs in all of the two-page spreads, and I've reproduced four of these in (11). These consist largely of categorical, bald assertions about matters of business practice that the business people addressed by the pamphlet would have special knowledge of. These assertions lack overt modality, hedging, markers of tentativeness and politeness. And some of the assertions are likely to be face-threatening for readers, some of whom presumably do for instance spend time and money trying to persuade customers to take what they've got (see (a)). And some of them are likely to be crashing truisms for the great majority of readers – e.g. the essence of marketing is to provide your customers with what they want in (a). Why is is that neither type of threat to face is mitigated? Why are these assertions bald on record? One answer might be that this is an expert-client relationship, and experts are allowed to say such things without mitigation. I don't find that convincing – most experts surely do mitigate especially when their audiences are established professionals. I suggest the baldness is more to do with identities: specifically, the enterprising self is one who is self-reliant, does not need to be pampered, can face up to things, can tell and be told straight. The style here is a metaphor for the enterprising personality. The DTI *qua* expert is constructing itself in the personality, and constructing it also as a subject position for the business reader. Furthermore, just as Young's speeches combine the discourses of enterprise, consumption, skill etc., so the DTI brochure combines the genres of expert-client interaction (as in 11), advertiser-consumer interaction (illustrated in 12) – there's a contrast between these two genres in that the DTI is 'authoritor'' in the former but 'authoritee' in the latter, so correspondingly advertiser-consumer interaction involves an attempt to persuade; and the traditional public service genre of service provider/service user interaction (illustrated in 13). As a result, the reader is placed in a composite subject position, as entrepreneur, consumer, client, and service user.

**Identity functions in language and discourse:
Implications of the Enterprise Discourse study.**

I want now to make some suggestions and comments about attending to identity functions in linguistic analysis, discourse analysis and semiotic analysis. I shall refer to identity functions rather than 'the' or 'an' identity function, though in fact I wonder whether the systemicist interpersonal function ought not to be seen as subdivided into an identity function and a relational function.

Identity functions in linguistic analysis

I want to look at the DTI pamphlet example in terms of probability modalities in Halliday's sense. Such modalities have traditionally been thought of in terms of speaker truth assessments of propositions. In recent work (e.g. by Coates, and Hodge & Kress), it's been suggested that people also use probability modalities for relational reasons: one reason for saying to your doctor *I think I've probably got flu* is not that you're unsure, but that you're deferential. What I'm suggesting is that, in the DTI pamphlet, a reason for categorical assertions without overt modalisation is the construction of social identity. So modality has identity functions too. In my forthcoming *Discourse and Social Change*, I've suggested that a doctor's use of subjective modality markers in a consultation (e.g. giving an opinion in the form of *I think that's wise* rather than *that's wise*) is to do with projecting a non-authoritative, lifeworld or maybe counselling identity. In the same vein, the doctor's communicative style manifests something like what Irvine calls 'conspicuous disfluency' and what Bourdieu identifies as 'the hesitant, even faltering, interrogative manner' of the 'new intellectuals'. What all this suggests is that probability modalities and allied phenomena are multi-functional. And it may be that there are other areas of grammar whose identity functions have been similarly neglected, And as the mention of conspicuous disfluency implies, prosodic and paralinguistic levels are potentially rich areas. Another area of interest here with both lexico-grammatical and prosodic-paralinguistic dimensions is meta-discourse and irony, where the text producer differentiates levels within her text and distances herself from some levels – interesting and problematic material for accounts of the subject as merely positioned in discourse.

Identity functions in discourse analysis

A first observation here is that one important reason for seeing textual analysis as a combination of linguistic analysis and discourse analysis is that discourse analysis highlights how different discursive practices construct social identities of different sorts. By discourse analysis I mean analysis which identifies genres and discourses drawn upon and the configurations they enter into in the production or interpretation of a text. Secondly, what the enterprise culture study drew attention to was the importance of attending to *orders of discourse*, especially in relation to the diffusion of cultural change in discourse. By orders of discourse I mean the totality of discourse practices within a social field or institution, and the relationships and boundaries between them. One can also think in terms of an order of discourse at a higher societal level, and the boundaries and relationships between these institutional orders of discourse within it. The enterprise culture example drew attention to distributional channels along which enterprise discourse, and discursive constructions of the enterprising self, can pass, linking politics to media and education and social services etc. But there is more to be said about orders of discourse, and that entails going beyond the limitations of the enterprise culture study.

Identity functions in discourse:
Limitations of the Enterprise Culture study

Identity functions in discourse analysis (continued)

One limitation of the enterprise culture study is that it is exclusively 'top-down' and concerned with attempts to engineer identity, without looking at how people respond to such attempts. Some preliminary observation of pressures towards identity change in higher education suggest that people respond actively, in many cases accommodating, containing or resisting change from above. For example, university prospectuses do now draw upon advertising and marketing models, but in academically modulated forms. Putting it in more general terms, while the positions and practices for social identity are socially handed down, people are able to negotiate their way among and between these models to varying degrees, and to use given resources to transform them (along the lines suggested by Bhaskar). This connects with critiques by for example Dews, Fraser and Giddens of theories of the subject which overstate the positioning and fragmentation of subjects, and understate agency and action: the work of constructing a coherent narrative of self-identity out of the diverse social resources available, as Giddens puts it.

Here again, the concept of order of discourse is important. It allows for diverse discursive practices to be drawn upon in creative combinations which redraw the boundaries between them and ultimately can transform the order of discourse itself. Indeed, this is already there in the enterprise culture example, in the combination of genres I pointed to in the DTI pamphlet for instance. In sum, discourse analysis and the order of discourse can account for both the social positioning of subjects in discourse, and the capacity of agents to creatively draw upon repertoires of discursive practices in constructing their identities, and in the process to change discursive practices and orders of discourse.

Identity functions in semiotic analysis

Another limitation of the enterprise culture study is that it does not take account of the combination of different semiotic modalities which is involved in constructing identities. For example, Emerson 1970 describes the construction of a medico-scientific ethos in doctors carrying out gynaecological examinations as involving setting, quality of gaze, and dress, as well as properties of discourse and language. A semiotic approach is important in understanding the limitations and obstacles facing attempts to engineer identity, whether by technologists of discourse or well-meaning social scientists: social identities are embedded in multiple naturalized and automatized dimensions of behaviour and are difficult to shift. A semiotic approach also links to the question of degrees of investment is social identities (discussed in Henriques et al 1984) and degrees of commitment to them. An important contemporary aspect of this issue is the problem of, and indeed crisis of, authenticity in social identity, associated perhaps with the unprecedented scale of cultural engineering.Authenticity is a problem for those who are subjected to cultural engineering as Hochschild points out in the case of air hostess – the problem of 'who am I?' – and for the publics who are faced with engineered identities in business and services – the problem of 'is this for real'. A challenge for linguists and discourse analysts is to shed light upon the capacity of people to distinguish the real from the engineered where they appear to be able to do so, and the places where they sometimes can't. Semiotic analysis, and attention to relationships, matches and mismatches between different semiotic modalities, may prove a useful resource.

Deconstructive and reconstructive perspectives

A further and more political challenge for critical linguists and discourse analysts is to turn analytical or in a broad sense 'deconstructive' work on social identity in a 'reconstructive' direction. This was a major theme of Halliday's presentation to the 1990 AILA conference. Identity problems and crises are a major feature of the contemporary world, be it crises of national identity or crises of identity in for example political groups (such as the contemporary left in Britain). Or again, people way beyond the ranks of the green movement are rethinking their identities as 'consumers' (or perhaps becoming more resistant to being constructed as consumer by others). It is perhaps not too fanciful or ambitious to think that an understanding of the role of discourse and language in identity construction and change may have a contribution to make. This would seem to be, or ought to be, a strand in the proposal for an 'ecolinguistics' made at the 1990 AILA conference – a form of critical linguistics focusing upon deconstructing unecological, technocratic and consumerist elements in contemporary discourse and language, and exploring the possibilities for reconstructing language and discursive practices for an ecologically oriented age. I would however endorse Halliday's cautionary note that 'we cannot transform language: it is people's acts of meaning that do that'.

Conclusion

What I am suggesting then is a more sustained focus upon identity in language and discourse as a way of equipping linguists and discourse analysts to play their part in work on cultural change. Specifically I have suggested that (a) grammar and other levels of language need some reworking to highlight identity functions – modality is one example; (b) a dynamic approach to discourse analysis, centering upon shifting boundaries between discursive practices in orders of discourse, can provide an account of social identity in discourse which neglects neither the social positioning of subjects nor the creative capacities of agents; (c) finally, a semiotic approach sensitive to the relationship between diverse semiotic modalities may shed light on obstacles to as well as possibilities of 'changing the subject' as well as issues like authenticity.

And linguistics and discourse analysis can be resource, as I have said, for both deconstructing and reconstructing social identities.

Appendix 1

Definitions of 'enterprise'

(1) By *enterprise* I mean the ability of an individual to create goods and services which other people will willingly consume. *Enterprise* meets people's needs and that is the source of jobs. (CPS 1/86)

(2) *Enterprise* encompasses flexibility, innovation, risk-taking and hard work – the qualities so essential to the future of our economy and our nation. (FR 7/85)

(3) *Enterprise* means an acceptance of personal responsibility and a confidence and desire to take action to improve your own circumstances. (BL 3/86)

Meanings of 'enterprise'

(4) Jobs come when *enterprise* has the freedom and vigour to meet the demands of the market, to produce the goods and services that people want (EE 3/85)

(5) The task of government (is) to produce a climate in which prosperity is created by *enterprise*. (EE 3/85)

(6) Attitudes which regard *business, enterprise and the job of wealth creation* as a positive benefit to society. (EE 3/85)

(7) Competition provides the spur to greater efficiency. Incentives provide the spur for *individual initiative and enterprise*. (EE 3/85)

(8) The Technical and Vocational Education Initiative, the National council for Vocational Qualification and Open College strengthened those links and raised the *skills and enterprise of individuals;* (BIM 11/87)

(9) Last April I asked chief executives to pledge their companies to recognise the *professionalism and enterprise of their managers* as a key to business success. (BIM 11/87)

(10) I hope the same will happen in management education and development so that we can fully use the *talents and enterprise of people* (BIM 11/87)

Orientation sections

(11)(a) The essence of good marketing is to provide your customers with what they want. Not to spend time and money trying to persuade them to take what you've got. So, whether you're selling at home or abroad, it's important to understand both the market and your competitors.

(b) Look behind any successful business and you'll find good design. While knowing your market can help you find the product or service your customers want, only good design can translate it into something they will want to buy.

(c) It doesn't matter how much time and effort you put into marketing, design and production. If the product or service doesn't live up to your customers' expectations, you're wasting your time.

(d) Long term planning is not a luxury confined to the larger companies. It is essential for any business which is to survive and compete in today's market place. (*The Enterprise Initiative* DTI 1988)

Genres

(12) Over the past few years, we've helped hundreds of small businesses to enlist the help of specialist consultants. We're convinced that it's the most cost effective way for a firm to help itself. So convinced, in fact, that we're planning to support around a thousand consultancies each and every month.

The (Enterprise) Counsellor will keep an eye out for the untapped resources, inefficient work systems and unrealized potential. You will get impartial (and, of course, confidential) advice based on the Counsellor's considerable experience. Only then will he or she recommend how their Consultancy Initiatives can best help you (DTI 1988)

(13) *Who qualifies?*

If you're an independent firm or group with a payroll of fewer than 500, the Enterprise Initiative offers financial support for between 5 and 15 man-days specialist consultancy in a number of key management functions. (DTI 1988)

References

Bernstein, B. 1990 *Class, Codes and Control vol 4*, R.K.P.
Bhaskar, R. 1979 *The Possibility of Naturalism*, Harvester.
Bourdieu, P. 1991 *Language and Symbolic Power*, Polity Press
Dews, P. 1987 *Logics of Disintegration: Poststructuralist Thought and the Claims of Critical Theory*, Verso
Emerson, J 1970 'Behaviour in private places: sustaining definitions of reality in gynaecological examinations', H. Dreizel (ed) *Recent Sociology 2*, Collier-Macmillan
Fairclough, N. 1989 *Language and Power*, Longman
Fairclough, N. 1990 'Technologization of discourse', Centre for Language in Social Life Research Paper, Lancaster University.
Fairclough, N. 1991 'What might we mean by 'enterprise discourse'?, in R. Keat and N. Abercrombie (eds) *Enterprise Culture*, Routledge.
Fairclough, N. 1991 *Discourse and Social Change*, Polity Press.
Fraser, N. 1989 *Unruly Practices: Power, Discourse and Gender in Contemporary Social Theory*, Polity Press.
Giddens, A. 1991 *Modernity and Self Identity*, Polity Press
Halliday, M.A.K. 1990 'New ways of meaning: a challenge to Applied Linguistics', AILA 9th World Congress presentation.

Henriques, J. 1984 *Changing the Subject: Psychology, Social Regulation and Subjectivity*, Methuen.

Hochschild, A. 1983 *The Managed Heart: Commercialization of Human Feeling*. U. California Press.

Hodge, R. & Kress, G. 1988 *Social Semiotics*, Polity Press.

Irvine, J. 'Registering affect: heteroglossia in the linguistic expression of emotion', in C. Lutz & L. Abu-Lughod, *Language and the Politics of Emotion*, CUP/Editions de la Maison des Sciences de l'Homme.

Thibault, P. 1991 *Social Semiotics as Praxis*, Minnesota U.P.

Cultural Studies for Advanced Language Learners

Ana Barro, Mike Byram, Hanns Grimm, Carol Morgan, and Celia Roberts ,Thames Valley University and University of Durham

Introduction

The purpose of this paper is to present a case for the systematic development of understanding of foreign cultural practices as an integral part of language learning for students at an advanced level. The case will be argued above all by demonstration of experimental courses in upper secondary and higher education. We shall begin however with a brief exposition of the standpoint from which we approach the development of methods and materials.

Foreign language teaching as education

Although it could be argued that the advances in language teaching in the past two decades have sprung from the clarity of purpose and techniques of language for specific purposes, it is important to remember that most language teaching takes place within the context of general education in schools or higher education. The work of the Council of Europe team (Van EK, 1984) has been influential in establishing syllabuses and methods according to an analysis of adult learners' needs. The development on a global scale of English for specific purposes has also had an effect on general language teaching. Yet, though 'needs analysis' can focus syllabus design, and teachers' and learners' objectives in the classroom, it remains evident that foreign language teaching has a role in the general, liberal education of young people, in preparing them for adult life in an internationally orientated society, wherever they happen to live.

This standpoint is reflected in policy statements and official syllabuses or curricula in many countries, in both advanced and

Graddol, D , L. Thompson
and M. Byram (eds) (1993)
Language and Culture, Clevedon:
BAAL and Multilingual Matters

developing societies. In particular two major purposes for language teaching can be discerned in such documents:

- language teaching shall equip learners with a practical ability, in both spoken and written forms of the language, to communicate with speakers of the language.
- language learners shall become, as a consequence of their exposure to foreign languages, more informed about and more receptive towards the people and societies associated with the language they are learning.

Unfortunately there has been a tendency to focus on the first of these as if it is separable from the second – which it may well be in the teaching of languages for specific purposes when such purposes are technological. In addition to the influence from LSP, the focus on the teaching of *practical* language skills is explicable as a contrast to earlier methods which gave excellent knowledge of the grammar and vocabulary of a language – and an ability to use it in the reading of the literary and other cultural artefacts produced in the written language – but very little capacity to use the language in interpersonal exchanges and face-to-face interactions.

This separation is however unfortunate for two reasons. First, any notion of communication which goes beyond the exchange of information has to take note of speakers' – and writers' – knowledge of the values and beliefs shared by the language community in question. This was the point made by Hymes (1971) in his extension of the definition of language competence to embrace the notion of 'communicative competence', – a notion therefore, that has its origin in anthropology. Hymes' definition was focused however on native speakers' interaction, the communication achieved by two or more speakers of the same speech community. When we consider interaction between a native and a foreign speaker – or of two foreign speakers from different language communities – it becomes evident that a further dimension has to be added. For when people with different cultural experiences wish to communicate they cannot assume that what they wish to say can be accommodated within the language and shared values and meanings of the native speaker of the language.(Gumperz, 1982) The foreign speaker may wish to take on the cultural world of the foreign language but cannot expect simply to abandon his/her own cultural world. He/she needs to be aware of the differences – and similarities – which have to be overcome in communication across cultures. For this reason, we need to recognise a further, *intercultural* dimension to communicative competence and not imagine that 'practical communication' can be separated from an acquisition of understanding of and receptivity towards other cultural and social practices.

The second reason for regretting separation of the two principal aims of language teaching relates to the process of learning about and tolerance of other societies and cultural values and beliefs. The assumption that if practical skills are 'taught', then understanding of others will be 'caught' is not justified. Many teachers can adduce their own experience of learners being unaffected in their ethnocentric and even xenophobic attitudes, and there is also some research evidence to support them.(Byram, Easarte-Sarries and Taylor, 1991) This suggests therefore that if language teaching is to attain its purpose of contributing to learners' general education, there has to be a systematic approach. And it is to the development of systematic approaches that the two projects to be described below are devoted.

One further point needs however to be clarified first, and this is that, unlike the grammar of a language, the complexity of value and beliefs embodied in the language of a social community is too great to be taught in entirety in a course of study at school or in higher education. Furthermore, such value and belief systems are subject to change and challenge. It is necessary therefore to provide learners with two kinds of knowledge and skill: a selected body of knowledge about the foreign language community and its shared values and beliefs, and the attitudes and skills for acquiring further knowledge as required in changing communication circumstances. The two projects described below put different emphases on these two dimensions of knowledge and skills and attitudes in accordance with the stages and contexts of learning involved.

The West London Project 1

This project focuses on preparation for residence in the foreign language community which is part of undergraduate language studies in all institutions of higher education in the United Kingdom. It is during this time that learners may acquire an insider's experience of social and cultural practices and thereby a fuller understanding of the beliefs and values expressed through and constructed in the foreign language. The project takes as its model the approaches and techniques of the ethnographer, traditionally a researcher who attempts to understand and

interpret the cultural world of a social group by living within it, as
a participant in its daily life, for a substantial period of time. (Agar
1980 Hammersley & Atkinson 1983) As language students also
become participants in a foreign language community, the model
seemed appropriate and, with the help of a professional
anthropologist, Brian Street, the project consists of the
development and trialling of a course in ethnography for
undergraduates in the year before their residence abroad.

It is however also one of the aims of the project that such a
course should be taught by language teachers who are themselves
not specialists in ethnography. In this way the project can, we
hope, become a normal part of undergraduate courses. The two
teachers who volunteered to join the team had therefore to be
both teachers on the course and themselves learners studying the
concepts and techniques of ethnography. Constraints of space do
not allow us to describe the whole process and we have decided to
concentrate on specific issues we consider of general interest at
this interim stage of reporting; the project runs from November
1990 to May 1993.

From a group of 10 volunteer students, we have chosen Gary
for a case study. Such a brief case study can provide only a
glimpse of the experiences and changes perceived by both students
and teachers involved but in the ethnographic spirit of the whole
project, it can illuminate the particular orientation of one student
in his own context. Gary was an 'average' student, neither the
keenest nor the most reluctant. He, like the others, showed initial
resistance to what were, in his words, 'mind-boggling ideas'
when we discussed, for instance, what gift-giving or the
construction and maintenance of social boundaries can tell us
about a particular set of cultural practices. Yet, within a relatively
short time, he came to grips with several concepts and techniques
for approaching a community 'from within'. using the vehicle of
ethnography.

We adopted a twofold approach on the course, involving on
the one hand discussion of key concepts drawn from social
anthropology and sociolinguistics; and providing, on the other
hand, opportunities to practise ethnographic methods of data
collection, namely fieldwork, participant observation and
interviewing. These two strands fuse in the simultaneous
development of reflexivity and awareness of methodological
issues.

Towards the end of the course, students were asked to do what
we called a 'home ethnography'. This involved doing fieldwork on
the students' home ground, during the Easter holidays. Gary

decided to study a group of close, mainly male, friends who also work for his father, who runs a small welding business in Bradford. His primary interest was in exploring the social roles and cultural models of this particular group of working class males and how they include and exclude others.

Though this was a project of modest scope and dimensions (a 3000 word essay done over the Easter vacation) he began to look in a more analytical way at the dominant discourses and interactional styles of his social circle, and started to categorise them according to how they perceived their social worlds. He also related them to broader anthropological concepts eg the social construction of cultural values, focusing on what it means to be a 'hard man, how solidarity is managed, and what all this might suggest about what it means to be a 'northern working class male'. Obviously his work raised many more questions than could ever be discussed in such a short time. Perhaps the most valuable lessons learned by Gary and the other students were about asking good questions, eliciting good quality data, and using anthropological concepts in order to unravel the cultural meanings. Thus Gary learned to rely more on his own observation of reality rather than on unmediated or perceived knowledge and in the process he became aware of at least some of the stereotypes which had previously conditioned some of his perceptions and responses.

What relation does this bear to the experience of residence abroad? The way we see it is that by studying interactions and the value systems constructed out of them, that Gary had previously taken for granted, he developed skills and an awareness of cultural processes which he can use and develop further when abroad. By using them to carry out an ethnographic study in Spain he would be motivated to develop his linguistic and intercultural competence.

Such enhanced awareness and sensitivity would help maximise his perception of what is culturally specific and also minimise 'culture shock'. Gary found it useful to get hands-on experience in his own environment, albeit in a modest way, before going abroad. The practice of 'making strange' in order to make the strange familiar, of really trying to 'get inside the heads' of people, was an essential part of his development. The following extract illustrates some of the cognitive and emotional effects of this process – a personal and intellectual challenge whether at home or in a different cultural setting.

After a failed attempt at my original title, I was rather stuck for some other topic on which to base my study. The ideal was to choose a group of people to which I had unlimited access and which I could observe without being conspicuous or influencing their behaviour. The obvious solution was to observe my friends. Although rather reluctant at first, as I thought nothing ever happens, after three weeks of 'making strange', close observation and many a drunken night out running off to the toilets to scribble down notes on beer mats, I eventually learnt that there was much more happening than what met the eye, and that I did not know these people as well as I thought.

This paper is mainly centred around the way in which people organize themselves into groups. By groups I mean to say a collection of people who are drawn together due to their common factors, such as interests, obligations, aims etc., and which are characterised by their own image, values, attitudes, vocabulary and codes of behaviour.

Detaching myself from the normal routine has definitely changed my outlook. I have realised that we are not, as I thought, simply just one group of friends and acquaintances, but that we are all divided into groups and furthermore into sub-groups, each one endowing a member with an image to project, a role to perform and a code of behaviour. I now know that bad feeling, upset and jealousy are caused by being excluded from a group and by the presence of two or more groups in the same place. Even now, as more people are being met, membership is increasing and new groups are being formed whilst more people are being excluded. (Mortimer 1991)

Gary found that taking less for granted and developing a more critical and systematic approach, generated an unexpected amount of data for analysis. It is then problematised and related to broader anthropological themes. The student, in effect, is developing intercultural competence in a way that is meaningful to him. Seeing a cultural group from the 'inside' necessarily entails close observation of the fine-grained detail which usually remains 'invisible'. The following extract is an example of how Gary went about recording and analysing his data in a careful and open-minded way, linking language to the cultural models that underpin the social behaviour of his friends, and revealing the dynamism and complexity by looking at a small defined area in detail.

Another source of misunderstanding, confusion and conflict was the misuse of roles, which yet again is another example of group behaviour exercised out of context, that is to say, two members belonging to the same groups do not interact with the same group code of behaviour, when one carries out his role as a member of another group whilst the other fails to realize. For example, on the night of the engagement party, Andrew received a phone call from Derek to see if he was still going out with his sister. Andrew's reaction was, 'Bloody big brother rings up to check if I'm still going out!' On another occasion, Andrew was not very pleased when Lorraine spoke of something she was supposed to know nothing about as it was told in confidence to Derek, by Andrew: 'How the xxxx does she know that. It must be Derek. I'm not telling him anything again.'

Another such example is that when wanting to get in touch with me by telephone, Andrew would ring someone else to relay the message to me. All this simply to avoid ringing my house and running the risk of having to speak to my father, who Andrew can only see as having one role i.e. 'boss'. Having to speak to my father on the telephone would mean a complete reversal of roles, 'boss' would become 'friend's dad' and 'employee/welder' would become 'son's friend.'

Andrew would therefore prefer to keep everybody's role separate in order to avoid the distress which occurs when roles are misused – as this leads to a breakdown of group membership, of image, and consequently a loss of identity.

Several of the issues touched on in Gary's home ethnography (related to cultural identities) have since been analysed in more depth during his 6-month stay in Sevilla, Spain. He has narrowed down his research questions to an exploration of Sevillano aggression and community among two specific groups in Sevilla. He has also been deeply involved in the ongoing process of analysing his own roles and relationships as a participant observer, which is incorporated into the final research report. Like the other group members who are working on ethnographic projects in Andalucia, the initial encounter with 'the other' provokes feelings of disorientation followed by a rapid process of acceptance, 'the honeymoon period' and then a more critical approach. As one of the students commented, the whole process was noticeably accelerated in comparison with the experiences of other Year Abroad students, partly because they had already discussed these aspects before their departure and in a sense anticipated them. Although the initial bewilderment was thus greatly lessened the 'honeymoon period' was also short. As one student put it 'the rose-tinted glasses fall off very quickly'.

During their stay, the students have been visited twice by a lecturer, as part of the ESRC research. On one visit, Gary made the following comments 'we're living this ethnography project 24 hours a day, so we couldn't stop if we wanted to,... it's made me much more aware of not just *what* people are saying, but also of *how* they're saying it.' Also 'I've been casting my net wide to get a feeling for what I want to look at, which has made me do a lot more, talk to people a lot more and go to places I would never have gone to otherwise.

Looking for cultural patterns beneath the surface has taken Gary and his group beyond the stereotyping and negative comparisons with Britain and has also made them less romantic about the host society. The cultural learning developed through ethnography (formulating analytical questions; not accepting things at face value; a new focus for language development and a more critical awareness of their own roles and relationships) has helped them to live more intensely within the new community, to feel close to it and so more able to develop a critical appreciation of it.

In sum. the programme aims to provide a framework, through exercises such as the home ethnography, which students can use to unravel the strands of the shared cultural knowledge which inform their lives. This same framework, strengthened by the process of self-knowledge, can then be applied to less familiar social and cultural contexts during residence abroad. This also gives an added dimension to the skill-based focus of many degree courses, enabling students to move beyond technical competency to a fuller linguistic and cultural fluency. In a relatively short time, students like Gary can hone their observation skills and become more confident analysts of the cultural meanings to be discerned from ethnographic observation. They are learning to make sense of what is involved in approaching one's own, or another culture in a more positive and sensitive way.

An evaluation of the course suggests a number of noteworthy points, summarised as follows:

- the students who volunteered came to the course with a degree of curiosity which no doubt contributed to its success
- they found the course different from others and a welcome change but the novelty of the early sessions soon led to a genuine commitment to making it work for them
- their motivation was maintained by using a task-based approach, often taking students' primary experience and their own data for analysis -
- teaching and learning were a shared experience. Since the teachers were themselves learners, and openly so, the ethos created by a cooperative classroom process had a positive effect on group dynamics, no doubt in part a consequence of the 'halo-effect' of a pilot course

Clearly some of these points raise the question as to how transferable the course can be in the future and whether its success can be repeated in a course that is part of the mainstream curriculum.

A related question arises with respect to the teachers themselves. They have found it exciting and novel and some of their enthusiasm has clearly encouraged students too. They have found their own situation as learners has created a different learning and teaching environment, which has reduced the 'distance' between them and their students.

The nature and 'spirit' of ethnographic enquiry seems not only to require, but also to generate, the necessary commitment on the part of the teachers. Given the open-ended nature of ethnography, with different students collecting different data, no course can ever be a replica of a previous one. This should enable teachers to sustain their level of interest and to repeatedly recreate the dynamics required to get the student involved.

In summary the success of the course so far can be attributed to the following features:

- the emphasis on acquiring a conceptual framework for understanding cultural difference, rather than descriptive facts about them
- the pedagogical factor: an atmosphere of shared learning among students and teachers
- students' perception of the relevance of the skills and concepts to their understanding of their own and the foreign cultural practices by using an experience-based approach to social anthropology and sociolinguistics
- a supportive environment which enables students to cope more effectively with not only the intellectual but also the personal challenges of 'doing ethnography'
- any vulnerability resulting from the course being outweighed by the sense of group solidarity and support among the students
- follow-up support during the Year Abroad by lecturers and created by the group themselves meeting regularly

The final evaluation will of course have to come after the period of residence in the foreign country and the re-integration of students into the final year of their undergraduate course, but at the half-way stage we can confidently say that the students have started to live the ethnographic life.

The Durham Project 2

The purpose of the Durham project is to develop a systematic approach to teaching an understanding of cultural practices for upper-secondary students. It is planned as an extension of existing courses for the General Certificate of Education (Advanced level) which serves as the final examination for upper-secondary courses in England, and for the Baccalaureat which serves the same purpose in France. It is a joint project between the School of Education, University of Durham, and the Institut National de Recherche Pedagogique in Paris. It functions on the basis of two teams of teachers and researchers working in parallel in France and England and developing jointly their theory and methodology. The applications differ in the two different education systems where, in France, the foreign language is one of several subjects to be studied, whereas in England it is one of only three, and students specialise and focus their work. A second significant difference is in the size of classes: in France, between 30 and 40 and in England usually with a maximum of about 20.

In both countries however there is an existing and increasing tendency to teach 'non-literary topic' – as they are called in England – or 'civilization' , to use the French term. This can be illustrated by listing these non-literary topics – where the lack of a positive term is symptomatic of the dominance of literature hitherto – from the syllabus of the University of Oxford Examination Board:

Non literary topics
Candidates offering coursework may write on any aspect of the topics listed below; for candidates offering the written examination, questions will be set on the more detailed areas given in brackets after the main topic headings. These 'sub-topics', as well as the literary topics in Section A, will change from time to time. Main topic titles will be varied as necessary.
Non-literary topic titles – French
Aspects de la politique ou des actualitÉs françaises
(la France et les affaires étrangères, 1988-1990)
Les média et la communication
(les développements récents dans le domaine de la TV et du cable en France)
Problèmes sociaux contemporains
(la violence – causes, effets et solutions)
Développements scientifiques ou technologiques françaises
(les ordinateurs et la société contemporaine)
Un peintre ou un mouvement artistique
(l'Impressionisme)
La sauvegarde de la nature et de l'environnement
(les parcs nationaux et régionaux en France)

Une région ou une ville de France
(no detailed prescription)
Aspects de l'industrie ou de l'agriculture françaises
(le profil d'une industrie ou d'un secteur industriel)

To illustrate the situation in France we quote from the guidelines issued by the Ministry of Education, in which the purpose of one of the aims of language teaching at this level is defined:

> Au collège, l'élève a été mis en contact avec les réalités culturelles les plus immédiates des pays de langue anglaise. A travers les textes, les images, les situations, les documents sonores, les interventions de l'assistant, il a été intéressé à certains aspects de la civilisation et de la societé anglo-saxonnes. Ces données culturelles ont fait l'objet de réflexions à la mesure de sa curiosité et de discussions à la mesure de ses moyens d'expression. En Seconde, il s'agit de baliser un domaine culturel vaste, ouvert et varié, par des repères coordonnés, historiques, géographiques, économiques, politiques, scientifiques, sociaux, techniques et proprement culturels. Il ne s'agit pas d'imposer à l'élève un rigide cadre de concordances, mais de lui donner des moyens d'orientation, en mettant à sa disposition des références utiles reliées entre elles par un réseau de relations de toute nature, réseau souple, d'abord simple, progressivement plus complexe. Par rapport à ce systeme de références, l'élève placera en perspective les connaissances qu'il a déjà acquises et il ordonnera utilement celles qu'il va acquérir. (Ministere de l'Education Nationale, 1988:16-7)

This then is the basis of our work. The focus in this experimental stage is on developing and teaching a short course of approximately 50 hours over two terms in the penultimate year of study: in England, Lower Sixth and in France, Première. The French approach is to develop a number of independent 'dossiers' on selected themes. In Durham we have chosen the same five themes which we see as related and incremental, and from this point, given limitations on space, we shall focus on the English team's work.

The five themes are similar to some of the 'non-literary topics' chosen by examining boards. They build on students' experience of related topics at G.C.S.E. level, although this is very limited in scope. They were also chosen after considering themes common to a number of Sociology A-level syllabuses. Finally, they were put in the following order: family, education, work, social identity, politics. This order represents a development on several dimensions:

- from familiar to unfamiliar topics
- through the stages of socialisation into the culture(s) of a country
- from the more concrete to the more abstract
- from analysis of information already prepared and presented to acquisition of data collection and presentation skills

This reduced course includes both a body of knowledge and the development of skills in discovering and interpreting other cultural practices. Some of these skills are borrowed and adapted from ethnography and it is intended that students should acquire some of the conceptual apparatus with which ethnographers and others analyse and interpret other social and cultural practices. The general aims of the course have been formulated as follows: Students will acquire:

- empathy with French people and some feeling of what it is like to be French
- a body of knowledge about key aspects of French cultural practices
- ethnographic techniques with which to approach other cultural practices and the curiosity, openness and independence to want to do so
- a perspective on their own cultural practices,, allowing them to set it on an equal footing with other sets of cultural practices rather than assuming they are the norm
- some understanding of how and why cultural attitudes arise
- an appreciation of the link between language and cultural practices and an understanding of culture-specific verbal and non-verbal behaviour, and the ability to use these in a culturally appropriate way.

These general aims were agreed in the research team and then each of the teacher members took one theme, wrote the objectives and procedures for it, and collected appropriate material for the unit. This material includes some which is commercially available in language teaching textbooks or audio-visual media, some which was collected in France, and some which was developed for the project; the latter consists mainly of recorded and transcribed interviews with young French people. In order to illustrate how the general aims are realised in specific objectives, we quote the objectives for the first and last units:

Unit 1: FAMILY
1 Students shall become aware of traditions in France, understand names/ceremonies and reflect on customs in Great Britain.
2. Students will be given information about different types of family which exist in France and will reflect on the nature of their own family life.
3. Students shall understand the way the state influences family life in France and Great Britain.

4. Students shall understand the significance of family meals and mealtimes in French family life and will reflect on attitudes in Great Britain.

Unit 5: POLITICS
Objectives: students shall acquire an understanding of:
1. politics and power structures operating in the relationships between individuals in any social group.
2. how, in society, these structures are embodied in formalised institutions.
3. some processes by which individuals wield power and of the operation of political institutions.
4. principal structures and institutions in the French political system.

The procedures and materials developed to realise these objectives vary from unit to unit, as students acquire skills in collecting and interpreting data from French people and from their own surroundings. The procedures have in common a comparative dimension and an attempt to help students to see a part of the foreign culture as insiders. In the unit on 'family', for example, we collected from a group of young French people an overview of the 'family occasions' during a typical year and the composition of the groups gathered under the label of 'family'. One such overview is shown overleaf

After studying this and similar documents, and beginning to establish the meaning of 'la famille', students were asked to write their own overviews, which were then compared and contrasted with the French ones.

This short illustration indicates some of the essentials of the methodology:

- to use data collected from native-speakers
- to use a data-collection technique in the students' own environment
- to analyse the cultural concepts from the insider viewpoint
- to compare and contrast – and thereby to relativize – aspects of the two cultures.

The selection of aspects of each theme is essential, given the time constraints. It is intended that, when this short experimental course is expanded to a two year course, each theme can be treated more fully and other themes added.

chez des amis les enfants et les parents dans 2 salles différentes	31 décembre	Réveillon de l'an
réunion de famille chez les grands-parents	1 janvier	Jour de l'an.
on mange la galette des Rois avec notre famille.	6 janvier .	Epiphanie
on invite la famille à la maison. (les grandsparents, les cousins, les oncles et tantes).	23 janvier	Anniversaire de ma soeur Julie.
on invite la famille à la maison. (les grandsparents, les cousins, les oncles et tantes).	12 mars	Anniversaire de mon père Phlippe.
Fin des cours	Fin juin	Examens de fin d'année scolaire
Passage des chars décorés pour la fete du 14 juillet dans le village	13 juillet	Soirée la veille de la Fete Nationale.
Jeux organisés pour les enfants du village suivi d'un bal de soir	14 juillet	Fete Nationale repas à la salle des Fetes du village.
Bal le samedi, le dimanche et le lundi soir	tous les ans la 1ère semaine du mois d'aout	Fete du village - manège, jeux
A 8 heures	10 septembre	rentrée scolaire
on invite à la maison mes grandsparents, mes oncles, mon parrain, mes cousins et mes cousines	30 septembre	mon anniversaire
on invite à la maison mes grandsparents, mes oncles, mon parrain, mes cousins et mes cousines	9 octobre	anniversaire de mon frère Antoine

(Stéphanie 16 ans)

Aspects are selected to illustrate what we consider to be essential knowledge about the theme, to offer opportunity for comparative methodology, to introduce students to data collection and interpretation and, not least, to provide attractive teaching materials.

There are other dimensions of the project which we have to omit here. In particular there is the issue of developing means of assessing cultural learning in forms which can be used by examining boards. There are also arrangements for evaluation within the team and by one of our colleagues from the Paris team. Finally, we link our classroom work with fieldwork. Ideally this consists of a period of 2-3 weeks residence organised by the school/college. Students have home-to-home exchanges or work placements. In other cases they may go on holiday visits. Whatever the circumstances, for each unit of classroom work there are proposals for corresponding fieldwork: participant observation, interviewing, small-scale questionnaire survey, keeping a field diary and a personal diary to chart their own observations and personal reactions to their environment. Some of these techniques are prepared in class – for example questionnaire design and analysis in the unit on regional identity. We have also had a day course focused on techniques, in which students designed a questionnaire, discussed observation techniques and watched video-recordings, and designed an interview schedule which they used to interview native speakers during the day.

Implications for future practice

One characteristic common to both West London and Durham projects is the fact that none of the teachers involved have any specialist knowledge of ethnography or other social sciences. It is one of the overall aims of this work to show that this need not be a hindrance to curriculum development which moves from 'literary' to 'non-literary' topics. The opposition is in fact unfortunate as, in the Durham project at least, the course materials include literary texts, and the project methodology transforms earlier practice by introducing literature both as a vehicle for understanding another culture and as a valuable cultural artefact.

In the longer term, the desirable situation would be that students from the West London project would become teachers who teach the kind of course developed in the Durham project. In the shorter term, it will be possible to use the West London project course – with some modifications – as the'basis for in-service training for those teaching 'non-literary' courses, which would be better named 'cultural studies for advanced language learners'.

References

Agar, M. (1980) *The Professional Stranger*. New York: Academic Press.
Byram, M., Esarte-Sarries, V. and Taylor, S. (1992) *Cultural Studies and Language Learning: a research report* . Clevedon: Multilingual Matters.
Gumperz, J. (1982) *Discourse Strategies* . Cambridge: Cambridge University Press.
Hammersley, M. and Atkinson M. (1983) *Ethnography: Principles in practice,*. London:Tavistock.
Hymes, D. H. (1971) *On Communicative Competence*. Philadelphia:: University of Pennsylvania Press.
Ministère de l'Education Nationale (1988) *Anglais: classes de seconde, première et terminale*. Paris: Centre National de Documentation Pédagogique.
Mortimer, G. (1991) *Member of the Group*. Unpublished.   Home Ethnography Project: Polytechnic of West London.
Van Ek, J.A. (1984) *Across the Threshold*. Oxford: Pergamon.

'I am a Creole, so I speak English.' Cultural ambiguity and the 'English'/Spanish bilingual-bicultural programme of Nicaragua's Atlantic Coast

Jane Freeland, Portsmouth Polytechnic

Introduction

This paper is based on work in progress on language politics and policies affecting the ethnic minorities[1] of Nicaragua's Atlantic Coast since the 1979 Sandinista revolution. Important stages in the development of these policies were the addition to the 1980-81 Literacy Crusade of mother-tongue streams in Miskitu, 'English' and Sumu, the Coast's three minority languages, and the establishment between 1984 and 1991 of 'bilingual-bicultural' education in those languages. This has been severely hampered by the surrounding conditions: an economy crumbling under counter-revolutionary attack; embargoes on trade and aid; under-development of the regional infrastructure; and shortages of trained human resources.

The Creole programme has also run against a reef of deep-seated ethno-cultural attitudes related to the ambiguity of the Creole cultural identity, and is threatening to sink under the contradictions. By exploring these, I aim also to explore some indirect relationships between language and culture.

Who are the Creoles?

Nicaragua's 25,000 Nicaraguan Creoles, or Afro-Caribbeans, constitute the third largest of the six ethnic groups comprising the costeo population. They are chiefly concentrated in the south of the Atlantic Coast, constituted since 1987 as the South Atlantic Autonomous Region (RAAS). They speak an English-based Creole, known to linguists as Mosquito Coast Creole (Holm

Graddol, D , L. Thompson
and M. Byram (eds) (1993)
Language and Culture, Clevedon:
BAAL and Multilingual Matters

1978,1983,1988) or Nicaraguan English (O'Neil (1991), Shopen (1987)), and to Creoles simply as 'English'. For now I shall adopt the Creoles' usage and unpick it later in this paper.

This usage, and the modern Creole identity of which it is a sign, are a product of the Creoles' slow rise and rapid fall in the ethnic hierarchy of the Coast, itself determined by the shifting patterns of Atlantic Coast history.

Two related processes have driven this history (Dunbar Ortiz (1984), Freeland (1988), Hale (1987), Gordon (1987)). The first is the rivalry between the Hispanic culture of Nicaragua's Pacific Coast and the 'Anglo' culture of the Atlantic Coast, since Spain colonized the Pacific Coast in the 16th century, and England occupied the Atlantic Coast in the 17th; both aimed to control this strategic territory, until 1914 the preferred site for an inter-oceanic canal. Constant attempts by Pacific Coast Nicaragua to integrate the Atlantic Coast into a Nicaraguan nation-state ruled by Pacific Coast Mestizos were met by equally constant resistance from different groups of *costenos* to what they perceived as annexation. This historic resistance was at the root of early conflict with the Sandinista Revolution, a product of the Pacific Coast Mestizo political culture.

The second process is a constant shifting of relationships between the ethnic groups of the Coast, triggered by the interventions of Britain and other external agencies, and of the Nicaraguan state. Different interventions privileged different groups, altering relations between them all, and giving rise to the complex of inter-ethnic divisions and rivalries which characterizes *costeno* society today.

Britain set the pattern by forming a strategic alliance against the Spanish with the Miskitu Indians of the Coast, and in 1687 recognising a Miskitu as 'King of Mosquitia'. Through this alliance, the Miskitu gained hegemony over the other Indian groups (the Sumu and Rama).

In the 18th century, the lower echelons of the ethnic hierarchy so created were swelled by African slaves, imported to work the British plantations and lumber trade. These were the ancestors of the present day Creoles. As in other Caribbean slave societies, colonizers and slaves interbred and their offspring and other favoured slaves were helped by their masters to acquire land. They eventually came to form a small mixed-blood elite within the black population, who adopted the name 'Creole' to denote their identification with their European forebears. Over time, this group was augmented by freed, escaped and emancipated slaves from other parts of the Caribbean.

During a brief hiatus in the British presence (1787-1821), the Creoles flourished, and began to take a measure of political and economic control. They became the Miskitu King's most influential advisers, leading merchants to the indigenous communities, and the 'torchbearers of English civilization on the Coast.' (Gordon 1987:137).

Political, economic and cultural developments in the 19th century enabled them to consolidate their position, replacing the Miskitu as the favoured group in the ethnic pecking order. There were three main strands to this process.

1 The Moravian Mission, which from 1849 began evangelizing first Creoles and later the Miskitu and other Indians, played a crucial role. Moravian English language schooling, unsuccessful among the Miskitu (Mueller 1932), gave the Creoles literacy and strengthened links with English-based high culture. Creoles from these schools were obvious candidates for training as 'native helpers' to the white missionaries, and later as ministers. As the Moravian Church became one of the most stable and powerful institutions on the coast, Creoles gained considerable authority, especially among the Miskitu.

2 The allied pressures of Nicaraguan nationalism (following independence in 1821) and US claims under the Monroe doctrine to exclusive influence in the Americas, gradually forced Britain to yield political control, ostensibly to the Nicaraguans, but in reality to their United States allies. In 1860, Britain ceded part of 'Mosquitia' to Nicaraguan rule in the Treaty of Managua. The remainder became a North American-style Mosquito Reserve, officially self-governing except in external affairs. Here, too, the Creoles gained the ascendancy: though the Miskitu 'king' retained nominal control, real political power lay with his Creole advisory council (Rossbach and Wunderich 1985).

3 From around the 1880s, US companies increasingly penetrated the Atlantic Coast economy, establishing virtual enclaves to extract its prime materials. The enclaves gave Creoles further opportunities for advancement. Heavy labour needs were met by Mestizo migrants from the Pacific Coast, casual Miskitu and Sumu wage-labourers, and unskilled black labour imported from the anglophone Caribbean. Creoles, with their English literate skills, became the clerks and middle managers.

By the 1890s, Creoles were firmly in the ascendancy, in the Church, in the Mosquito Reserve, and in the enclave labour hierarchy. However, their authority was not entirely their own; like the Miskitu before them, they exercised it as mediators of British or North American power.

It was also short-lived. In 1893 Pacific Coast political developments brought to power the Liberal President Zelaya (1893-1910), determined to unify the Nicaraguan state economically and culturally. When the Creole leadership defended the autonomy of the Reserve, Zelaya militarily occupied its capital, Bluefields. Spanish-speaking Mestizos replaced Creoles in government and economic administration, and a policy of cultural Hispanization imposed Spanish over English as the region's official language, outlawing teaching in other languages. Far from achieving national unity, the Reincorporacin (as it was officially known) fuelled hostility to 'the Spanish', particularly among Creoles.

Though the ban on English-medium education was lifted on Zelaya's deposition, the Coast remained under Nicaraguan jurisdiction and Spanish remained the official language. Indeed, the Somoza dynasty (1936-1979) undertook a new and more consistent drive for 'spiritual nationalization', imposing Spanish as the medium of instruction throughout the school system, with few concessions to the multilingual nature of the region.

In the labour hierarchy of the enclaves, however, Creoles retained their status rather longer. Indeed, the name 'Creole' came to distinguish a lighter-skinned, older-established, more 'middle-class' group from 'Negroes', the immigrant black workers, and this distinction persisted until well into the 20th century (Mueller 1932:57,Conzemius 1932:7). Eventually, 'Negroes' assimilated 'upwards', until the designation 'Creole', with all its connotations, applied to all Afro-Caribbean costeos.

As the enclaves declined and US companies withdrew, this status too was gradually eroded. By the time of the Sandinista triumph, Mestizo-run Somocista enterprises had largely replaced North American capital, a corrupt Mestizo bureaucracy had cornered both political and economic power, and Mestizo migration into the region had demographically overwhelmed all other groups. Creoles now occupied a precarious middle position in the ethnic hierarchy of the Coast (see Fig. 1).

Reading upwards from the bottom of the hierarchy, Creoles were a clear cut above the Rama, Garfuna, Sumu and Miskitu. They engaged only reluctantly in the agricultural labour and commercial activities associated with these groups and with the Mestizo peasantry, continuing to aspire to the professional, clerical and artisan positions associated with their traditional status. Indeed, Creoles did objectively hold a disproportionately high share of such jobs, through their judicious use of such educational opportunities as existed, especially those afforded by the Protestant schools (Gordon 1985); there was also a significant group of Creole intellectuals and professionals, often educated in the United States.

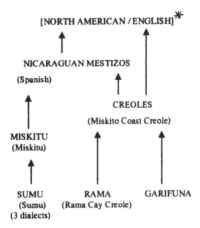

* The direct presence of this layer disappeared immediately following the revolution, though its cultural presence remained.Arrows show direction of pressure to assimilate, +/ bilingualism

Fig. 1: Nicaraguan Atlantic Coast ethnolinguistic hierarchy –1979

Others migrated, internally from rural areas to Bluefields or to Managua, and externally to the USA. Most Creole families had at least one member sending dollar remittances from the US. They could therefore afford the imported foodstuffs, household articles and clothing which are essential elements of their material culture, but are generally associated with an upper-class life-style in the rest of Nicaragua.

Reading downwards from the top of the hierarchy, however, Creoles were clearly subordinated to the Mestizos, who held the leading posts in government, business and the professions, and who despised Creoles as *negros* (though both groups manifest a wide range of physical types). Nevertheless, Creoles still perceived themselves as the natural elite of the Atlantic Coast, regarding the Mestizos as inferior, poorly educated usurpers. In a modern version of the old Anglo-Hispanic rivalry, they aligned themselves with the 'Anglo' culture of Britain and the United States, in opposition to the dominant 'Hispanic' culture.

In other words, the Creole identity had become a highly ambiguous cross between a class and an ethnic position, grounded in an idealized memory of their former status as an economic and cultural elite, favoured by the now absent English-speaking colonizers. Materially, it was not attached to land, like the Indian cultural identity, but to a place in a particular socioeconomic hierarchy dependent on a specific set of economic conditions.

In particular, few Nicaraguan Creoles would define themselves as Black, or identify with the Black nationalism of the period. Marcus Garvey had been influential in Bluefields in the 1920s, and had heightened Creole ethnic consciousness, but his influence had confirmed rather than broadened the specifically Nicaraguan Creole identity. The same is largely true of the Southern Indigenous and Creole Council, a Creole cultural revival movement, formed in 1977 under the auspices of the Moravian Church (Vilas 1989:92-3), though its dissemination of the ideals of Martin Luther King inspired some young Creoles to take pride in their blackness.

Identity and language

The ambiguity of the Creole cultural identity is precisely reflected in the state and status of their language. Before the *Reincorporacion* of 1894, the makings of a post-Creole continuum (DeCamp, 1971) existed in the Mosquito Reserve: English-medium schooling supported English, the lexifier language, and there was a significant community of native acrolect speakers. By analogy with other Anglophone Caribbean countries, it seems likely that upward social mobility, and the distinction between 'Creoles' and 'Negroes', would correlate with command of a greater range of the continuum, though this is not described in the literature.

The withdrawal of institutional support for English in favour of Spanish, and the gradual departure of the native acrolect-speaking community eroded this continuum. Nevertheless, though there is evidence of relexification of Mosquito Coast Creole (MCC) Spanish (Holm 1978), Spanish did not replace English, but instead reduced it to a tenuous and highly idealized presence. By the 1960s, it was maintained only by the Protestant Churches and schools, especially the Moravian College, which taught it as a curriculum subject, bending the rules on Spanish-medium education by teaching some classes in English. Only Standard English (SE) was permitted in the classroom; Creole was 'broken English', and harshly corrected. Whilst this is a common Caribbean phenomenon, it acquired a peculiar acuteness in this context, where the College became a citadel defending English as a kind of High language in exile.

Creole speakers of SE were a dwindling minority: according to a 1985 assessment, '40 or older, educated in the Colegio Moravo of Bluefields when English was taught by North Americans or US-educated Nicaraguans' (Yih and Slate 1985:26), or in the USA. Almost by definition, they were prosperous, urbanised, middle class. Nevertheless, all Creoles still identified themselves as 'English-speakers'. 'I am a Creole, so I speak English' is not so much a linguistic statement as a declaration of cultural allegiance and opposition to the dominant, Spanish-speaking culture.

This polarization clouds certain linguistic realities. For the idealization of English to work, Creole must necessarily be relegated to the status of a 'dialect'. At the same time, for Creoles, Miskitu and Sumu alike, Creole carries reflected prestige which belies this status, from its association with 'English', the Language of Wider Communication, preserved in the Moravian College, taught as a foreign language in all Nicaraguan schools, and valued as a passport to jobs in the USA. Effectively, Creole is English.

In reality, Creoles operated within a complex polyglossic system, involving Spanish, an idealized (and, it should be emphasised, indeterminate) SE, Mosquito Coast Creole, Miskitu, and Sumu.

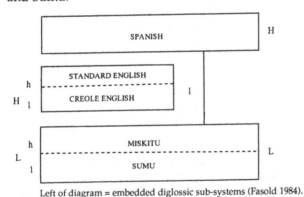

Left of diagram = embedded diglossic sub-systems (Fasold 1984).

Fig 2: Nicaraguan South Atlantic coast Polyglossic system

For the sake of accuracy, this diagram incorporates the diglossic relationship between Miskitu (h) and Sumu (l) which cannot be elaborated here, but see Freeland (in preparation).

Spanish was indisputably the High language of the region: the official national language, obligatory medium of instruction in schools, and of interactions with the state; 'English' was as low a language as Miskitu and Sumu. As the ingroup language of the Creoles, 'English' (denoting Creole) stood in a diglossic relationship to Spanish rather than to SE, with which the majority had virtually no contact. Indeed, few commanded the full range from basilect to acrolect: Moravian educated speakers of SE abandoned their basilect; some Spanish- educated basilect-speakers commanded various points on the mesolectal scale, most used the basilect. Normally, the shift from lower to higher language functions was into Spanish. Only the few SE speakers could also perform these functions in SE, and opportunities to do so were relatively restricted.

Mother tongue education

The Sandinistas came to power with a commitment to liberate the peoples of the Coast. They planned to develop the Coast's economy, end ethnic and racial discrimination, and 'encourage the flowering of the local cultural values of the region which derive from the original aspects of its historical tradition' (FSLN 1969). These commitments stimulated rapid mobilization of most groups around ethnic rights, notably the right to bilingual education in 'mother tongues' and Spanish. In 1980, 'Literacy Year', literacy programmes in Miskitu, English and Sumu were added to the National Literacy Crusade, and a Law on Education in Indigenous Languages was passed, authorizing transitional bilingual education in Miskitu or English with Spanish up to fourth grade of primary school (JGRN 1980). However, growing tensions with the Miskitu and their escalation into counter-revolutionary war curtailed adult literacy programmes and held up the application of the law until 1985, when it was extended to include the Sumu.

For all groups, 'mother-tongue' was identified by consulting speakers themselves. In the case of the Miskitu and Sumu, the choice was unproblematic. These are 'mother-tongues' according to all four of Skutnabb-Kangas' (1981) defining criteria: first language, best-known language, most-used language, and language of internal and external identification (except perhaps for Sumu acculturated towards Miskitu but wishing to re-identify as Sumu). The Creoles, however, opted overwhelmingly for SE, their 'mother-tongue' chiefly by extremely strong internal identification (their external identification as native speakers by SE native speakers is problematical). Nevertheless, their choice of SE as the language of literacy made perfect sense: it is the

Language of Wider Communication and power to which most English-speakers, Creole heritage or not, want access. Choice was also motivated by Creole expectations that 'ending racial repression' meant recognizing their former status, of which education in SE was an essential ingredient.

This second purpose became particularly clear when in 1983 the minorities began putting pressure on the government to implement the 1980 law on bilingual primary education. Like the other groups, Creole advocates pleaded the 'mother tongue' case: early learning in the first language was more efficient, facilitated the transition to Spanish, and would increase ethnic pride. Yet the Creole documentation is also notable for the prominence of economic arguments for SE – as a resource, for the country and individual speakers – and for its tendency to blur the distinction between 'the Creole dialect' and SE (Yih and Slate, 1985, Hurtubise, 1990). Only a few dissidents argued that to teach SE was 'to impose an alien language and culture on the students, as is happening now with Spanish... [or] that it would be a surrender to cultural domination by historic oppressors.' (Yih and Slate ibid.).

The conflation of SE and 'mother tongue' caused relatively few problems for the Adult Literacy Crusade, though it should be emphasised that a full evaluation was never made. The manuals were designed by a 'Technical Team' of linguists and teachers, some from the Moravian College, to lead learners from spoken Creole towards the syntax and lexis of simple written English. Technical advisers from the US, Belize and Grenada helped *brigadistas* deal with problems on the ground. Even so, there were difficulties: most of the *brigadistas* were Creole High School students whose formal studies had been in Spanish, and who were not entirely literate in English. Had the campaign gone into a follow-up phase, difficulties might well have become more acute. As it was, adults seemed to accept that this was 'proper English', and bound to be different.

The real contradictions emerged with the bilingual-bicultural programme for school-children. Indeed, its development has been a dialectical process of discovering, and resolving through experience, the sociolinguistic realities of the Coast and the place of Creole within them. Every stratagem for avoiding Creole has brought the programme closer to it. From our cultural and professional perspective, we might argue that this process should have happened through a pilot project rather than by experimentation with the whole education system. Indeed, this was the original proposal: a four-year pilot designed by a professional team, to run in a selection of schools in three different areas. It would include teacher training, and 'recognize the differences... between Creole English and SE in order to identify the forms known to a child of six and the words where these forms are most frequent.' (Brooks 1984). The decision to implement a full school programme was considerably influenced by the feeling it would command stronger government support. Indeed, it is arguable that only when English education spread beyond its elitist strongholds could the sociolinguistic realities fully emerge.

The programme's first strategem, to satisfy the 'mother-tongue' condition that children should learn to read what they can say, was to teach children to speak SE in pre-school and first grade, and then to read. This approach can work with adults, whose language repertoire is already formed, especially if it is linked to discussion of the situational appropriateness of both varieties (Figueroa 1985). For children in particular, it carries a hidden message that Creole is unacceptable which undermines the spirit of the programme. Moreover, the effort to speak SE where Creole would be natural violates community speech rules, and sets up a new 'High' language function (SE = School English!). Had it worked, it would have perpetuated the Moravian School practice, and the acute linguistic insecurity to which many of its graduates confess.

Fortunately, it failed. Like the Literacy Crusade *brigadistas*, most teachers had been formally educated in Spanish. Few had encountered the whole of the post-Creole continuum, so could not be good SE models and felt uncomfortable trying. Moreover, in parents' eyes, it unacceptably delayed the onset of literacy teaching.

This strategy was therefore abandoned for one which assigns Creole to oral work and reserves SE for literate skills. This eases classroom communication: in the classes I visited, teachers moved freely between Creole, for talking to the children, and various mesolectal approximations to SE, for reading. It also restores stylistic appropriateness. But the gap between spontaneous speech and written language remains unbridged; there is no space for children to start writing as they speak; teachers tend to emphasize formal correctness, rather than content. Such problems are not absent from our own classrooms, whose teachers familiarly read and write English. These teachers learned to write in Spanish, and feel extremely inhibited about writing in English. (In Bluefields' bilingual newspaper, *Sunrise*, even the most gossipy and colloquial English pieces are translated from Spanish.) Consequently, there is a tendency to 'do it by the book', seeking safety in mechanical methods: teaching procedures are 'whole class repetitions of readings, drills in the form of cloze activities and written copying of readings.' (Hurtubise 1990).

A 1988 evaluation of Creole reading skills showed that these methods, too, were failing: 76% of 3rd– and 4th–grade children were barely literate (Hurtubise 1990). An obvious next stage, identified by some of the programme's tcnicos, is to admit some form of written Creole. At present there is still widespread resistance to this idea. Linguists from outside have promoted it in vain (Shopen, 1987, Hurtubise, 1990); attempts by MIT's 'Linguists for Nicaragua' to run workshops preparing Creole materials failed; the materials were never used, perhaps because they forced the pace of change. Advocates within the community are generally young, Sandinista sympathisers, and identify themselves as Black; their voices do not yet carry far. As one of them put it: 'I think that we haven't learned to love our own selves as Black people with our own language.' (Nidia Taylor, popular cultural worker, interviewed March 1991). Nevertheless, they form the nucleus of a movement to re-value Creole involving an oral history project and poetry writing in Creole, SE and Spanish.

Much of the resistance centres on this designation of Creole as a 'language' rather than a dialect of International English. Linguists and young Creoles promote it to emphasize the validity of Creole: it is systematic, can be written, has cultural autonomy. For the majority, however, such autonomy signals a potential loss of status: if Creole is a language, 'mother-tongue' education could be used to ghettoize Creoles, not advance them.

These contradictions will only be unravelled when the programme has a well-trained, authoritative teaching force. At present, as 'empirical' teachers whose chief authority lies in being members of the Creole community, they are in the worst possible position: lacking confidence in their own spoken and written SE, untrained to analyse their 'language / dialect', a prey to conflicting theories and attitudes. They need a good grounding in applied linguistics, with a strong sociolinguistics component, to enable them to situate Creole socially and historically, and explain it to pupils and parents. Since there is no tradition of linguistics or anthropology in Nicaraguan universities, this means foreign technical assistance.

Before the electoral defeat of the Sandinistas in February 1990, clear-sighted evaluations of the programme (MED 1989), and plans for new training modules for bilingual teaching strongly suggested that the process of learning by experience would continue. Unfortunately, bilingual education comes low in the new government's priorities; since the changeover it has been starved of support and its future is now in jeopardy. If, at this vulnerable moment in its development, the programme has to be defended from first principles, defensive positions will be adopted, which will paralyze this process.

Note

1   The terms 'ethnic group', 'indigenous group', 'people', and 'nation' are all sensitive in the debate on minority rights in Nicaragua. I use 'ethnic group' here to include dominant and minority groups, and to avoid the connotations of 'aboriginality' carried by some of the others, which are particularly divisive in the Nicaraguan context. For these reasons, this is also the term used in the Nicaraguan Constitution (1987) and the Atlantic Coast Autonomy Law (1987). For a different view, see Ortiz 1989:12). *Costeno* [of the coast] is used by and for natives of the Atlantic Coast region, of all ethnic groups, including Mestizos, particularly when defining themselves in opposition to Pacific Coast political initiatives.

References

Brooks, R. (1984) *El problema linguistico en Zelaya Sur: Alternativas.* in Hurtubise, J. (1990) Appendix 4.

Centre for Documentation and Research on the Atlantic Coast (CIDCA) (1982) *Demografia Costena: Notas sobre la historia demografica y poblacion actual de los grupos etnicos de la Costa Atlantica Nicaraguense.* Managua: CIDCA.

CIDCA (1987) *Ethnic Groups and the Nation State: the case of the Atlantic Coast in Nicaragua.* Stockholm: University of Stockholm / CIDCA.

DeCamp, D. (1971) Toward a Generative Analysis of a Post-Creole Speech Continuum. In Hymes, D (ed) (1971) *Pidginization and Creolization of Languages:349-370.* Cambridge: Cambridge University Press.

Dunbar Ortiz, R. (1984) *Indians of the Americas: Human Rights and self-determination.* London: Zed Books.

Figueroa, J.J. (1985) Language and How we Use It. In Craven, J and Jackson, F. (1985) *Whose Language?: A Teaching Approach for Caribbean Heritage students.* Manchester: Manchester Education Committee – The Central Manchester Caribbean English Project.

Freeland, J. (1988) *A Special Place in History: the Atlantic Coast in the Nicaraguan Revolution.* London: Nicaragua Solidarity Campaign / War on Want.

Freeland, J. (in preparation) *Language and revolution on the Atlantic Coast of Nicaragua* [working title].

FSLN (Sandinista National Liberation Front). (1969). *Historic Programme.* In CIDCA 1987:70.

Gordon, E. T. (1987) History, Identity, Consciousness and Revolution: Afro-Nicaraguans and the Nicaraguan Revolution. In: CIDCA 1987:135-168.

Hale, C. R. (1987) Inter-Ethnic Relations and Class Structure in Nicaragua's Atlantic Coast: An Historical Overview. In CIDCA 1987:33-57.

Holm, J. (1978) *The Creole English of Nicaragua's Miskito Coast* London: University College, unpublished PhD Thesis.

Epitomized in:

Holm, J. (1983) (ed) *Central American English*. Hague: Julius Groos Verlag.

and:

Holm, J. (1989) *Pidgins and Creoles, Vol II, Reference Survey* Cambridge: Cambridge University Press.

Hurtubise, J. (1990) *Bilingual Education in Nicaragua: Teaching Standard English to Creole Speakers*. New Zealand: unpublished dissertation for Diploma in Education (insitution unspecified).

JGRN (Government of National Reconstruction) (1980) Law on Education in Indigenous Languages on the Atlantic Coast. In Ohland, K. and Schneider R. (eds) (1983) *National Revolution and Indigenous Identity: The Conflict between Sandinistas and Miskito Indians on Nicaragua's Atlantic Coast: 79-83*. Copenhagen: International Work Group for Indigenous Affairs.

MED (Ministry of Education). (1989) *Programa Educativo Bilinge-Intercultural: Investigacin Evaluativa 1984-1987*. Managua: Ministry of Education.

Mueller, K. A. (1932) *Among Creoles, Miskitos and Sumos: Eastern Nicaragua and its Moravian Missions*. Bethlehem, Pa.: Comenius Press.

O'Neil, W. and Honda, M. (1987) Nicaraguan English / El ingles nicaraguense. Wani: Revista sobre la Costa Atlantica 6, 49-60.

O'Neil, W. (forthcoming / 1991) Nicaraguan English in History. To be published in Hale, Ken (ed) *Linguistic Fieldwork: Case Studies from Nicaragua*. Cambridge University Press.

Rossbach, L. and Wnderich, V. (1985) Derechos indigenas y estado nacional en Nicaragua: la convencion mosquita de 1894. Encuentro 24- 25, 42-4.

Shopen, T. (1987) Some comments on the English-Spanish bilingual-bicultural education program in Zelaya Sur. / Algunos comentarios sobre el programa bilinge-bicultural ingles-espanol en la region autonoma del Atlantico Sur. Wani: Revista sobre la Costa Atlantica 6, 97-107.

Skutnabb-Kangas, T. (1981) *Bilingualism or Not: The Education of Minorities*. Avon: Multilingual Matters.

Vilas, C.M. (1989) *State, Class and Ethnicity in Nicaragua: Capitalist Modernization and Revolutionary Change on the Atlantic Coast*. Boulder and London: Lynne Rienner Publishers.

Yih, K. and Slate, A. (1985) Bilingualism on the Atlantic Coast: Where did it come from and where is it going? Wani: Revista sobre la Costa Atlantica 2-3, 15 & 43-47.

Cultural Orientation and Academic Language Use

Lixian Jin and Martin Cortazzi, University of Leicester

Introduction

In this paper we outline some major features of the cultural orientation of Chinese post-graduate students and visiting scholars studying in 6 British universities and 1 polytechnic, drawing on data gathered through questionnaires and interviews with a sample of 101 subjects. We focus on their experience and beliefs about academic culture, their expectations of learning and academic language use (ALU) and their orientation to tutor/supervisor-student relationships. This is contrasted with the cultural orientation of 37 British academic staff, who also completed questionnaires and were interviewed.

Culture is necessarily subjective and involves assumptions, ideas and beliefs which are often not articulated. Participants may not be explicitly aware of them. Culture is 'a set – perhaps a system – of principles of interpretation, together with the products of that system' (Moerman 1988 p.4). 'Every culture is also a structure of expectancies' (Kluckhohn and Kelley 1968 p.209). It cannot be assumed that principles of interpretation and expectancies of relationships, interaction, learning and language use – all key elements in academic culture – are necessarily the same for all those involved in ALU, most especially among overseas students. Here, the interpretations and expectations of Chinese students are contrasted with those of their tutors.

At a general level it is useful to consider language and interaction in relation to the cultural dimension of individualism versus collectivism proposed by Hofstede (Triandis 1990). This dimension – a cluster of attitudes, values and types of behaviour – has implications for students' learning strategies and for their use of language skills.

Graddol, D , L. Thompson
and M. Byram (eds) (1993)
Language and Culture, Clevedon:
BAAL and Multilingual Matters

Individual and collective tendencies

In individualist cultures people focus on 'I' for their identity, while in collectivist cultures they focus much more on 'we'. In individualist cultures people look after themselves and their immediate family only, whereas in collectivist cultures, people belong to in-groups or collectivities which look after them in exchange for loyalty (Hofstede & Bond 1984 p.419). Collectively-oriented cultures have been called 'high synergy societies' by the anthropologist Ruth Benedict and psychologist Abraham Maslow (quoted in Moran & Harris 1982 p.110, 1991 p.313) because they emphasize group consciousness, cooperation and mutual reciprocity.

If culture is a resource, people in every culture probably draw on both individualist and collectivist tendencies, but the relative emphasis varies. There is a tendency towards individualism in the West and towards collectivism in the East (Triandis 1990).

Chinese culture can be broadly characterized as collective (Hofstede & Bond 1984). This parallels Hsu's (1981) analysis in which the key to Chinese culture is that the Chinese are situation-centred: they see people in terms of relationships, conformity and mutual dependence according to the situation.

From the questionnaire results, 47.4% of the Chinese subjects confirmed that a Chinese person judges his/her behaviour mostly according to what people around expect, whereas only 19.7% of the British subjects thought that the Chinese would behave in this way. 91.8% of the Chinese subjects thought a British person judges behaviour according to his/her personal values, whereas only 65.8% of the British subjects believed this about the British.

Cultures emphasizing the collective orientation focus more on 'in-groups'. Individualist cultures have many specific in-groups but these exert less influence on individuals than the wider in-groups of collectivist cultures. Members of collectivist cultures tend to draw sharper distinctions between in-groups and out-groups: in-group relationships are seen as being more intimate and more important. When they are in Britain, Chinese students often relate to their home country or to the Chinese student community as the major in-group. They see themselves as a homogenous group, sharply distinguished from other groups: they are Chinese above all, belonging to the same group, even having the same level of knowledge. As an interviewee said, 'Chinese don't know many things, we know more or less the same. Among the Chinese, if I know everyone knows. If I don't, none of us does'

Tutor-student relationships

The interaction between British academic staff and Chinese students can be analysed in terms of the cultural expectations and interpretations which the two groups have of each other. In many respects their cultural orientation can be seen to be individual or collective. This distinction seems important to understand British academic culture, certainly from the Chinese perspective.

Broadly speaking, British academic culture is based on the notion that students will develop independence and individuality. Individuals are believed to have their own talents and abilities and these are developed in a system of higher education in which independent thinking and self-expression are emphasized. Alternatives should be considered to reach a balanced judgement and critical evaluations of arguments are expected, often resulting in differing individual conclusions. This is acceptable because many concepts turn out to be relative, especially in arts and social sciences, and because originality and creativity are valued – like independence, these are individualistic qualities. A fair degree of equality is expected in academic social interaction, such that students may disagree with academic staff, are expected to develop their own opinions and offer their own ideas. Staff see themselves as often learning from students, especially at postgraduate level. They acknowledge that they do not know everything in a particular area and may believe that it is not possible to do so.

A Chinese interpretation of academic culture is somewhat different. As might be expected from a collective perspective, social dimensions and relationships are key features. Students come to acquire knowledge and have very high academic expectations of supervisors, who may have international reputations. They seek guidance from their teachers, who are expected to be moral and social leaders, experts who know everything in their specific area and who can plan for and instruct students. The crucial relationship is that between teacher and student, which is seen in paternalistic terms. The teacher should tell students what is what and how to proceed. He or she should be one who is worthy of imitation. The teacher should be sensitive to any student problems and should be helpful in social and everyday issues arising out of living in another country. Like a parent, the teacher should care for students academically and socially.

Expectations

SUPERVISORS	CHINESE STUDENTS
Students should develop ...	*Teachers should provide ...*
independence	acquisition of knowledge
individuality	guidance
creativity	imitation, models for/of learning
openenness to alternatives	a single answer
processes of investigation	results and solutions
critical thinking	new methods to learn, ways to reach advanced technical levels
Students should ...	*Teachers should ...*
think for themselves	be moral leaders
know what to do	know everything in their area of expertise
express themselves when they need help	should ask students if they have any problems plan for and instruct students be sensitive, sympathetic, helpful and know our problems
take responsibilities academically, and for everyday activities	act as parent supporting children
mix with British	no money to go out with them

Orientations to language and culture

Chinese students and British tutors were asked about various aspects of the students' orientation to language and culture. The results show some interesting contrasts and asymmetrical perceptions.

The students were asked about their knowledge of the English language, British culture and the British academic system, which they had obtained from their teachers of English in China. Since the questionnaires were administered in Britain this reveals their retrospective reflections now rather than their current observations at that time. They were asked how confident they felt then about their knowledge of English grammar, pronunciation, vocabulary and about their knowledge of the British education system, culture, society and research methods. They were further asked about how useful or otherwise this knowledge was, now that they were in British higher education.

The figures below do not include neutral responses. The figures for students' confidence compared with the usefulness of this knowledge are all statistically significant by the Wilcoxon matched-pairs signed-ranks test. The significance for *all* items is *p=0.0000*, except for pronunciation which is *p=0.0005*.

	confident	little/no knowledge	useful	useless
English:				
Grammar	80.2%	9.9%	45.5%	14.9%
Pronunciation	51.5%	13.9%	71.3%	6.0%
Vocabulary	39.6%	16.8%	90.1%	1.0%
British:				
Education system	21.8%	53.4%	42.6%	23.7%
Culture	24.8%	40.6%	49.5%	21.8%
Society	19.8%	51.5%	52.4%	15.9%
Research Methods	17.9%	60.4%	70.3%	8.9%

The data illustrate great changes in perceptions of language skills and social, cultural and academic knowledge. Overall, the Chinese students, prior to departure, felt far more confident about their knowledge of language than they did about their knowledge of British culture, society, the education system and British research methods. Once here, vocabulary and pronunciation are perceived as being overwhelmingly more useful than knowledge of grammar, which most had previously felt confident about, but which turned out to be useless for a few. If needs can be expressed as what students feel least confident about but see as being most useful, their perceived need for knowledge of research methods is striking. Similarly, their need for knowledge about British society and culture is fairly strong. Tutors need to be aware of these perceptions.

In the same way, the Chinese students were asked about their confidence in using specific language skills prior to departure and how useful they now found them. The skills illustrated below are listening, note-taking, speaking, intensive reading (which is given some emphasis in English classes in China), skimming, scanning and writing research papers. The results are interesting, with statistically significant differences between the confidence and usefulness variables (*p=0.000*, except for Intensive Reading which is *p=0.0019*)

	confident	little/no knowledge	useful	useless
English language skills:				
Listening	42.6%	27.7%	95.1%	1.0%
Notetaking	13.9%	65.3%	72.3%	5.0%
Speaking	36.6%	36.6%	95.1%	2.0%
Int. Reading	37.0%	36.6%	72.0%	7.0%
Skimming	39.0%	29.0%	85.0%	2.0%
Scanning	37.6%	27.7%	86.2%	1.0%
Writing	24.8%	54.4%	86.1%	3.0%

There is a clear lack of confidence about these skills, particularly in view of the students' confidence about grammar (80.2%), yet they are overwhelmingly held to be useful. Given this, it might be supposed that the Chinese students would need some language help. Such help would be particularly appropriate with writing, where the students' need – in terms of the difference between confidence and usefulness – is greatest. Students were asked about how much help they expected, and how much they help thought they had actually received from their tutors (not from a language centre or from specialist language support staff).

Answers from students are compared those of tutors, who were asked how much help they thought their Chinese students expected and how much help they had, in fact, given them directly. The figures below are all in the category of 'some' or 'a lot' of help on the questionnaire and ignore figures for 'a little' or 'no help'.

	Students' View		*Tutor's view*	
	help expected	help received	help student expected	help actually given
English language skills:				
Listening	59.4%	53.5%	74.3%	72.9%
Speaking	61.3%	49.6%	64.7%	62.1%
Reading	48.5%	42.6%	60.0%	54.0%
Writing	68.3%	42.6%	77.1%	75.0%

More tutors thought that students would need help than students did. There is a significant difference ($p=0.0490$) with reading: 48.5% of the students expected help with reading, but 60% of the tutors had expected to give them help with this skill. Similarly, there are different perceptions regarding the help actually given – more tutors claim to have given direct help than students believe they received. The significant differences are with writing ($p=0.0021$) and listening ($p=0.00476$): 75.0% of the tutors maintained that they had given help with writing, while only 42.6% of the students said that they had received such help, although writing was their greatest need; 72.9% of the tutors said they had given help with listening compared with 53.5% of the students who had received it, although listening was the highest rated skill in terms of their confidence.

Students were also asked about their current language competence for the four skills and their tutors were asked to estimate the students' current competence. The figures below are for replies in the category of 'no problems at all' or 'quite competent' on the questionnaire, as opposed to 'not very good' and 'needing more help and practice'.

English language skills:	Students' view competent	Tutors' view competent
listening	53.4%	75.7%
speaking	46.0%	73.0%
reading	83.1%	86.5%
writing	46.5%	67.7%

Writing is the skill with which the lowest number of students feel confident, together (surprisingly) with speaking. Writing is also the skill on which fewer tutors rate the students as being competent. Again, there is a contrast between tutors' and students' estimations, with significant differences emerging between the estimations of the two groups for listening ($p=0.0216$) and speaking ($p=0.0147$).

Further differences in cultural orientation are shown in comments made in interviews. The quotations are presented in a format of a 'dialogue'. Such a dialogue should take place, but so far as we gather, has not happened in real life.

C=Chinese students/visiting scholars; T=British tutors

Individual/collective

C: There are differences between the two cultures; the ways of thinking are different too. I want to know from which angle they consider or think about a matter.

C: My supervisor said I should choose whatever I wanted.... But from a Chinese way of considering the matter, I think I should obey whatever they need... I am so used to this way of working, i.e. I am told what to do, to do the research according to the need of the authority. So now I feel very passive about choosing a research topic. But it seems to me that their way of considering a matter is that you choose what you are interested in.... But as for me, I feel very embarrassed to ask, because perhaps they do not need this aspect of research.... I don't know what they really think.

T: To give help with an individual piece of work all I can do is to offer the space in tutorials and encourage the students to talk about what projects they are up to, but I have to rely... and I choose to rely... on their sense of motivation, what interests them and what is important for them, not what is important to me.

In this 'dialogue', the Chinese student considers a matter from a collective point of view, whereas the British tutor sees the strength coming from the personal interest of an individual. The Chinese student obviously shows his criterion for choosing a research topic, which is based on the needs of others. From a British point of view, personal motivations would inspire an individual to devote him/herself to the work and therefore an individual's interest in the work is vital. It could be difficult for either side to change their way of thinking. But it would be helpful if both sides are aware of the differences of thinking.

Independent/dependent
The following quotations illustrate contrasted expectations between British tutors and Chinese students on the independence of working. However, some British tutors have realized that they need to give help to their students at the beginning of their study and Chinese students have also understood that they have to depend on themselves.

T: I think they learn, during the period they're here, that study is independent, that you're not just doing what someone tells you, and that you want to be creative.

T: The Chinese students really need a lot of steering, especially early on, but, once they've got going and they've got some confidence, then they're excellent, they really are.

C: Here we have to learn how to do things on our own. Our supervisors won't bother to tell us. But in China, our supervisors would guide us step by step to start the research and help us all the way through.

Asking for help/expecting the offer of help
In China, people expect to be offered help and to show care in a community. This is another aspect of collectivism. In Britain, generally, it is up to an individual to show the need for help, i.e. one normally has to ask for help in order to get it. Others who initiate help could be seen as intruders. These different ways of thinking may determine how they deal with the matter of help. The following quotations show the difference.

T: They don't tell me their problems as well as they ought to. They
        do tell you, but you have to goad it out of them, really.

C: ...he (supervisor) never asked me if I needed any help. Maybe
        they don't know what to do with us because of the differences
        between cultures and ways of thinking.

C: If you ask them for help, they seem quite friendly and helpful.
        But normally they wouldn't talk to you, ignoring you. It's very
        difficult to contact them.

Discourse patterns in writing

The two contrasted views in the following quotations on the style
of writing may indicate the reasons for difficulties and problems
that Chinese students have in English academic writing, as seen
by British tutors.

T   ...writing is certainly jumbled up in some ways. I've read so much
        of the things my (Chinese) students have produced and yet I still
        can't see a pattern... You can have, on one extreme, almost total
        Chinese proverbs, in a technical piece of writing... you can see the
        chap suddenly revert to a Chinese proverb to prove his point! It's
        rather nice, but you can't do that in a technical report, that's the
        trouble.

T: ...the style we encourage: main point at the beginning, then try to
        build up the paragraph, later to prove the main point or
        hypothesis, then give a summary or conclusion at the end.

C: I think the Chinese style of writing is helpful to deal with
        problems. The initial part is a foundation which is the reason for
        a request...

C: ...The Chinese style of writing is constructed with reasons and
        feelings. The conclusion comes from step by step reasoning. From
        Confucius' time, we have been told we must present a source and
        origin, otherwise the reasoning cannot be made clearly. There is
        no present without the past and origin. Therefore we should
        report from the root.

Tutor-student relationships

C: We generally wouldn't disagree with our supervisor's words or
        instructions, no matter whether they suit us or not....if they don't
        agree, they just keep silence or if they say something, they just
        hint a little bit, very implicitly. The majority are like this. Even
        the minority who are more straight forward, they wouldn't say
        something back straight, they say it round about.

C: In China you are supposed to listen to your supervisor. You have
        to care about the personal relationship with colleagues, about
        whether I'm going to offend others.

C: It's impossible to talk to him (supervisor) properly..... He is like a
        manager. Here the name of a supervisor is, in fact, a manager....
        This management is in charge of money.

T: I see my role as pushing responsibility back onto students. Your
        Chinese students look after your own interests.

T: ...they think tutors are up here (gesture) and they probably have
        difficulty in arguing with a tutor in the way that most English
        students would more readily.

It seems that these Chinese students use their expectations of a Chinese supervisor to deal with their student-tutor relationship in Britain. On one hand, they respect their tutors and are 'scared' of British tutors, as they would be in China. On the other hand, they do not receive parental care from their British tutors, as they would in China. This may create a double problem of relationship.

Acculturation and cultural synergy

In examining students' and tutors' cultural orientation and their ALU, Schumann's Acculturation model of SLA is a helpful framework (e.g. Schumann 1978, 1986). Acculturation involves culture contact and change: changes in the language and culture of a group occur as a result of interaction with a different linguistic or cultural group. In Schumann's view, it is 'the social and psychological integration of the learner with the target language group... any learner can be placed on a continuum that ranges from social and psychological distance to social and psychological proximity with speakers of the TL and... the learner will acquire the second language only to the degree that he acculturates' (1978 p.29). He sees acculturation in terms of the causal variables of social and psychological distance and each of these is made up of a number of factors:

Acculturation model of SLA

Social Distance
social dominance
dominance
  non-dominance
  subordination
integration pattern
assimilation
  adaptation
  preservation
enclosure
  high/low
intended length of residence
  short
  medium
  long

cohesiveness
  high/low
size
  large/small
congruence
  similar/dissimilar
attitude
  hostile
  neutral
  positive

Psychological Distance
language shock
culture shock

motivation
  integrative
  instrumental
ego permeability

The Acculturation Model was put forward to account for the SLA of subjects with lower or intermediate language levels acquiring language in non-instructional settings, i.e. their language levels and cultural levels, in terms of the TL culture, were low. However, the Chinese subjects in this research have high levels of competence in English (a minimum of 550 on TOEFL and 6.5 on ELTS tests) to start their study here. They are all successful academics or professionals who have strong motivation and clear aims for studying – in China they would be considered the cream of the intellectual elite. Learning strategies which they developed in China helped them to high academic success there. However, the same strategies used in the U.K. will not reveal their academic strengths in the context of British academic culture.

Despite high language competence their familiarity with British culture and society in general and with British academic culture in particular is low. Furthermore, on the British side, few academics claim any great knowledge of Chinese culture and society. There is a cultural gap but no question of SLA at basic language levels. This is nearly the opposite of the situation of subjects to whom the Acculturation Model is usually applied. Gardner (1985) has suggested, however, that it might be applied to foreign language learning. The Chinese subjects have learnt English as a foreign language but with little or no cultural input and limited contact with native speakers. Now, as advanced second language users in Britain they do not attend language classes, though some have attended a pre-sessional course. Further learning of English on their part is therefore through natural language learning in an SL setting via ALU.

The Chinese students do have cultural problems in Britain, including academic cultural problems. The concept of acculturation related to ALU is clearly relevant. Their tutors also have cultural problems in their interaction with the students. The element of congruence in the Acculturation Model refers to similarity or otherwise of culture between the SLL and TL culture. This is a one-way concept from the SLL to TL speakers. The acculturation is only considered from the SLL's point of view. Here, however, there is a need to consider the tutor's lack of cultural knowledge of the students' background and how this leads to a measure of misunderstanding which affects ALU. Naturally the tutors expect the students to move culturally towards them and to learn or fit into British culture. Yet the Chinese students have some expectation, from their own academic cultural background, that the tutors will move towards them: helping them, instructing them, and caring for them. Such expectations of mutual or reciprocal cultural movement suggest that a concept of cultural synergy (Moran & Harris 1991 pp.91-92) should be included in any framework applied to this case.

Cultural synergy means here that people from two or more cultures interact systematically, cooperating for a common purpose with an attitude of being willing to learn, understand and appreciate the other's culture without loss of their own status, role or cultural identity. In this concept, adaptation, rather than assimilation, is emphasized, otherwise it is likely that learners will fear that their original culture will be downgraded, which may create a psychological barrier to learning the target culture and language.

As a British interviewee put it,

> ...what you need to do, to benefit from the experience, is to try to pick out the best parts of the British way of doing things and at the same time resort to or retain the best ways from the Chinese, and then you might actually be benefitting in a way that no one who hasn't experienced both systems could do.

The Cultural Synergy Model thus involves the key notion of two-way acculturation which would mean that participants develop a mutual awareness and understanding of each other's culture: from SLL to TLS and vice versa. Cultural contact in the academic context should enable both sides to be aware of cultural differences. Seeking interpretations and explanations may well bring insight to their own as well as the other's culture. A progressive movement from both sides can be envisaged bringing gradual mutual congruence. This is a product of the process of synergy. The larger the cultural congruence – understanding of the other culture – between SLS and TLS the more effective the ALU. Cultural synergy in this context is a tool for learning: it is the major cultural role of second language use in higher education.

Conclusions

This research shows that both sides misunderstand each other. This seems to be because both groups have a lack of explicit cultural awareness of their own and the other culture and see the other's academic and social behaviour in their own terms. Often, when the British tutors and Chinese students attempt to communicate, linguistically and culturally, they seem to follow parallel paths. For the Chinese this often means a period of at least several months of academic and personal difficulty which they overcome by hard work but without, perhaps, understanding what the problem was. It may well be that many of the problems evident in these data could have been avoided by cultural knowledge on both sides. Mutual cultural awareness would enable participants on both sides to know what to expect. It is highly likely that the practice of cultural synergy between tutors and students would benefit students' ALU.

Some extensions to the Acculturation Model can be proposed for the case of the Chinese students, and perhaps other students:

- the model may be relevant to ALU, especially in instances of low acculturation, which includes the lack of knowledge of the TL culture and the TL academic culture;
- congruence needs to be thought of as mutual cultural congruence or a dynamic synergetic process. It not only refers to the existing similarity between the two cultures, but also to a movement from both sides to enlarge the overlap area between them. This movement can be achieved when participants become conscious of the differences in order to minimize the gap and increase the congruence;
- this concept of synergy does not mean the merging of two cultures into one; but means understanding the other culture, behaving appropriately in the other culture without losing one's original cultural identity.
- a collective-individual dimension needs to be added;
- academic culture shock should be included.

Such a model seems to fit both the British tutors' academic cultural context and the Chinese collectivist orientation. From the British point of view, it is a part of academic culture to consider alternative interpretations, perspectives and ways of thinking and this is exactly what many international students at advanced post-graduate levels may have to offer – varying and diverse perceptions of academic culture. Especially in social sciences, Chinese (or other groups), may thus constitute a human and intellectual resource which could be drawn on as part of the academic cultural process for the benefit of tutors. Teachers are also learners, after all. To ignore such a potential resource would seem to be at variance with British academic culture.

From the Chinese side, cultural synergy may be seen to accord with a collective orientation, involving as it does, deeply held ideas about group harmony, cooperation, reciprocal relations and learning. In a group of students, each one is potentially a teacher; as Confucius said, 'Where three people are gathered, there must be one who could be my teacher.' Coming from a high synergy society, it would therefore seem to be a natural step to be involved in cultural synergy for ALU. To take this step would involve some reconsideration of in-group and out-group boundaries.

References

Gardner, R.C. (1985) *Social psychology and second language learning: the role of attitudes and motivation.* London: Arnold.

Hofstede, G.; Bond, A.M. (1984) An independent validation of Hofstede's culture dimensions using Rokeach's value survey. *Journal of Cross-Cultural Psychology.* **15**: 417-433.

Hsu, F. (1981) *Americans and Chinese, passage to differences.* Honolulu: University of Hawaii

Kluckhohn, C.; Kelley, W.H. (1968) The Concept of Culture. In A.Dundes (ed.) *Every Man his Way, readings in cultural anthropology.* Englewood Cliffs: Prentice Hall

Moerman, M. (1988) *Talking Culture, ethnography and conversation analysis.* Philadelphia: University of Pennsylvania Press.

Moran, T.; Harris, P. (1982) *Managing Cultural Synergy.* Houston: Gulf Publishing Co..

Moran, T.; Harris, P. (1991) *Managing Cultural Differences.* Houston: Gulf Publishing Co.

Schumann, J.H. (1978) The Acculturation Model for Second Language Acquisition. In R.Gingras (ed.) *Second Language Acquisition and Foreign Language Teaching.* Arlington,VA: Centre for Applied Linguistics.

Schumann, J.H. (1986) Research on the Acculturation Model for Second Language Acquisition. *Journal of Multilingual and Multicultural Development:* **7**:379-92.

Triandis, H.C. (1990) Theoretical Concepts that are applicable to the Analysis of Ethnocentrism. In R.W. Brislin (ed.) *Applied Cross-Cultural Psychology.* Newbury Park: Sage.

Projecting a Sub-Culture: The construction of shared worlds by projecting clauses in two registers

Susan Hunston, University of Surrey

The issues addressed

This paper plays a small contributory role in the discussion of two issues: that of evaluation and that of register. In this introductory section, therefore, I shall give a brief overview of these issues.

Stubbs (1986) has made a plea for what he calls a 'modal grammar' of English: a description of language use that will take into account the attitude or evaluation that is encoded in every utterance. He notes some of the multiplicity of ways in which a speaker or writer can modify an utterance in order to convey not only information but an orientation towards or opinion about that information. Such a study explores the interrelation between grammar, lexis and pragmatics and must be, as Stubbs' title suggests, 'a matter of prolonged field work'.

One of the many complexities facing the researcher in this area is the various kinds of opinion that may be given in an utterance. I have proposed elsewhere (Hunston, 1989) that evaluation be perceived as operating along three separate parameters: certain-uncertain, good-bad and important-unimportant. Here I shall concentrate on the first of these parameters. I shall examine one way in which speakers/writers express their assessment of the degree of certainty afforded to each proposition.

The expression of degrees of certainty is important in at least two respects. Firstly, in registers which construct knowledge, such as scientific papers, the status of a proposition as it is offered by the writer to the scientific community is crucial to the way in which the proposition can then be treated by that community. As an illustration, consider the following invented sentences:

- *It has been assumed that the dichroism is negative.*
- *It has been found that the dichroism is negative.*
- *It has been proposed that the dichroism is negative.*

A subsequent researcher, wishing to challenge this writer's work, for example, would be constrained to deal very differently with

Graddol, D , L. Thompson
and M. Byram (eds) (1993)
Language and Culture, Clevedon:
BAAL and Multilingual Matters

the *assumption*, the *finding* and the *proposal* respectively. As researchers travel further along the road from direct observation to theoretical conclusion, the status of their utterances becomes less certain and, as Pinch (1985) has observed, the utterances then play a different role in the construction of knowledge. (See Hunston, forthcoming, for more details of this point.)

Secondly, the assessment of certainty may be used, not simply between I and you as information-holders but between *I* and *you* as social beings. An assertion may be mitigated by apparent vagueness or lack of certainty in order to maintain face, to be polite (cf Holmes, 1982, Myers, 1989, Coates, 1988). Coates, for example, suggests that modal modifications of certainty are used to affirm non-threatening, solidarity relations among women. In a different context, Myers suggests that scientific writers use modal modifications of certainty to avoid being too face-threatening towards fellow researchers.

The second issue to be addressed in this paper is that of register. Although there are various theories of register/genre, they share a concern with the 'sameness' of texts produced in different times and places based on similarities of context, of style and of organisation. Evaluation, including evaluation of certainty, is important to a theory of register because different registers, being informed by different ideologies, should show evidence of different value systems. It seems likely, then, that different registers will express the assessment of certainty in different ways.

Some support for this hypothesis has come from a previous study (Hunston 1991) in which ways of expressing epistemic modality were compared using Halliday's categories of Subjective Explicit, Objective Explicit, Subjective Implicit and Objective Implicit (Halliday 1985:332-4). Texts from three registers were used: research articles, newspaper editorials and discussions on the radio programme 'Any Questions'. This study showed that although there was considerable variation between the texts, especially the editorials, there was greater similarity within each register than between the registers.

The most clear-cut cases – the research articles and the radio discussions – have been taken as the focus for this study. The texts selected for analysis consist of five articles from the journal *Language in Society*, each from a different year (1985-1989), each reporting experimental work, and five texts from the Radio 4 programme 'Any Questions', each text comprising all four of the monologues answering a single question.

The isolated feature

The literature on the modification of certainty is not small, and concerns mainly studies of modals (e.g. Butler 1990) and studies of a conglomerate of features often referred to as 'hedges' (e.g. Makaya and Bloor (1987), Prince et al (1982)). In this paper, however, I shall focus mainly on the method of modifying certainty exemplified in the invented examples above: clause complexes involving report verbs and other projections. In such clause complexes it is the report verb or similar that indicates the speaker/writer's degree of certainty, a phenomenon described most recently by Thompson and Ye (1991). Here, however, I shall focus on the subjects of these verbs.

The feature which I isolate for examination in this paper, therefore, is the kind of clause complex in which modal information concerning the central proposition of the complex is expressed, not as a modal verb or adverb in the clause containing that proposition, but as a separate clause. Examples are:

Example 1
It is certainly possible that the treatment was administered a little before or a little after the apparently definite time period. (FFF10)

Example 2
..a little thought shows that they [numbers] cannot be [exact]. (FFF11)

Example 3
Inspection of the Table shows that Session 5 differs from the others.(FFF32)

Example 4
I don't think Gorbachev and perestroika are finished but I think they're in great danger. (G4.36)

These exemplify what Halliday refers to as *Interpersonal Metaphor* (Halliday 1985, 332ff). The interpersonal information is expressed not congruently, using the modal system, but metaphorically, using a projecting clause. One of the key features of such metaphorical expressions is that the assessment of modal certainty is made explicitly objective (Examples 1-3 above) or explicitly subjective (Example 4).

I have included in my data several classes of example which Halliday would not, as I understand it, include as interpersonal metaphor. The most important class is projecting clause complexes which report what other people have said e.g.

Example 5
He [John Major] said that that issue would not be when but whether (ME11)

Here I am arguing that the choice of report verb in such a clause complex allows the speaker/writer to indicate an attitude of agreement or otherwise towards the proposition, and that this also stands as a metaphorical expression of modality (cf Thompson and Ye, 1991; Hunston,1989).

I also include nominalisations of projecting clauses and inserted clauses with or without *as, according to* . Examples are:

Example 6
There is some evidence that points to a possible over-generalization from the Japanese linguistic system. BAC21

Example 7
At the same time, Mizutani says, the non-Japanese themselves disturb Japanese speakers by failing to give frequent responses. BAC5

Example 8
..the Japanese concept omoiyari, which, according to Lebra (1976), is a key concept for understanding Japanese people. BAC31

My justification for taking projecting clauses for study is that, uniquely among expressions of judgement concerning degree of certainty, they also assert the source of such a judgement. In Example 4 above, for instance, the source of the judgement is acknowledged to be *I*, whereas in Example 3 it is *Inspection of the Table*. (This may be glossed as *the table gives evidence of the truth of this proposition to anyone who cares to inspect it.*) In Example 2, the source is what might be called *common sense*, whilst in Example 1 there is no source: the judgement is unattributed. In Example 5, *John Major* is the authority for the statement.

It seems reasonable to suppose that this attribution of the source of a judgement is not random but that it reflects the construction of a shared world between writer/speaker and reader/hearer. In that world, it must be acceptable to propose either John Major, or common sense, or the speaker's own self as the basis upon which a judgement may be made and believed. One observes in Example 3 an ideology in which tables speak for themselves and in Example 2 an appeal to a shared perception. It seems reasonable as a consequence to hypothesise that, as the shared worlds of registers must differ, so what may occur, and what occurs most frequently, as the source of such assessments of certainty will also differ.

Findings and discussion

Quantitative data from all texts

The first task is to identify the subjects of the projecting clauses, hereafter referred to as the sources of judgement, and to classify them into types. The classification can be expressed as a set of networks, as in Figure*1* which has been arranged so that the primary distinction made by it - between self and non-self - coincides with Halliday's categories of Subjective and Objective respectively. The other distinction is between attributed or non-attributed as types of non-self source. Further details of the non-self attributed sources are expressed as a network in Figure*2*. Here the primary distinctions are between people and entities (events and states) and between entities which exist external to the text and those which are introduced to the reader/hearer by the text itself. This category of 'internal' will be further glossed below.

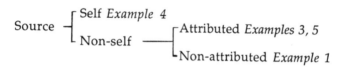

Figure 1: The general source network

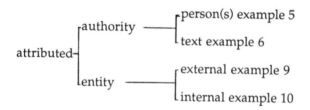

Figure 2: Non-self: attributed network

Here are further examples to illustrate the figures:

Example 9
Studies of human nonverbal communication have suggested that social status relationships, social bonding, and willingness to comply are indicated in gaze direction, facial expression, body posture, and tone of voice (refs). (DUM 28)

Example 10
The findings presented in Table 1 show that the frequency of use of listener responses is culturally specific...(BAC 15)

The occurrence of each of these sources in the texts is as follows:

	non-attr	attrib self		total
SC	0	5 (28%)	13 (72%)	18
G	3 (8%)	6 (16%)	28 (76%)	37
Th	8 (32%)	6 (18%)	20 (59%)	34
ME	0	9 (24%)	28 (76%)	37
HW	1 (5%)	4 (21%)	14 (74%)	19
total	12 (8%)	30 (21%)	103 (71%)	145

Table 1a: Occurrence of sources in Any Questions texts

	non-attr	attrib self		total
BAC	1 (3%)	31 (79%)	7 (18%)	39
DUM	7 (33%)	13 (62%)	1 (5%)	21
PRE	21 (26%)	52 65%)	7 (9%)	80
SUTY	5 (14%)	31 (86%)	0	36
FFF	5 (21%)	16 (67%)	3 (12%)	24
total	39 (20%)	143 (72%)	18 (9%)	200

Table 1b: Occurrence of sources in Language in Society texts

	person	text	external	internal	total
SC	4	1	1	0	6
G	2	0	2	0	4
Th	5	0	1	0	6
ME	9	0	0	0	9
HW	5	0	0	0	5
total	26 (87%)	0	4 (13%)	0	30

Table 2a: Non-self sources in Any Questions texts

	person	text	external	internal	total
BAC	15	1	0	15	31
DUM	6	3	0	4	13
PRE	13	5	0	34	52
SUTY	20	3	1	7	31
FFF	7	1	0	8	16
total	61 (43%)	13 (9%)	1 (1%)	68 (48%)	143

Table 2b: Non-self sources in Language in Society texts

I shall now discuss some of the most important differences between the texts and suggest how they may be accounted for in terms of the sub-cultures which produce the different registers.

Self versus non-self (Figure 1 and Table 1)

In the *AQ* texts, 71% of judgement sources are self; in the *LiS* texts, the figure is only 18%. Furthermore, the majority of 'Self' sources in *AQ* (85%) portray the self as *thinker*, as in Example 4. In *LiS*, the majority of 'Self' sources (63%) refer to something *said* by the writer at another point in the text, as in Example 11.

> Example 11
> *...I will demonstrate how these conventions change in cross-cultural conversations for American listeners, whereas they remain unchanged for Japanese listeners. (BAC34)*

Note that the certainty of the proposition is still being evaluated here, by the choice of report verb, but the self is portrayed as a text-constructor rather than as an opinion-holder.

The implications of these observations are these. Within the subculture of AQ, it is the opinion of the speaker which is held to be of value. It is assumed that world problems and events are subject to subjective interpretation. This interpretation is based solely on each speaker's internal world view. Furthermore, each personal judgement is of equal validity. This is suggested by the very layout of the programme, with each speaker in turn taking the floor for a monologue. There is no attempt to resolve discrepancies between the opinions of the various speakers, as consensus of opinion is not required.

Within the subculture of sociolinguistic experimentation, however, personal judgement is not valued for itself, and is indeed disguised as having another, 'Non-self', source. Judgements of probability are not attributed to I but appear to rise automatically from the data, as in Example 10, or are part of a construction of agreement regarding consensual knowledge, as in Example 9 (cf Hesse's 1974 view of scientific knowledge) It must be stressed that what is being implied here is more than a convention of objectivity in academic writing. I shall illustrate this with reference to a counter-example. In text FFF, the writer, Dubois, uses I with unusual frequency. In a prologue to the paper, the pronoun appears 21 times; but only one of these is the source of a judgement of certainty. Although FFF is in many ways unconventional - Dubois herself appears very much as an individual in it - the judgements concerning findings are still not attributed to her. Dubois may eschew some of the conventions of academic style, but she is still aiming to contribute to consensual knowledge.

To interpret the figures further, it is necessary to look again at Figure 1. It will be remembered that the network represented in Figure 1 was constructed to make salient Halliday's distinction between *Subjective* and *Objective*. It would be equally possible, using the same categories as in Figure 1, to construct a network in which the primary distinction was made between judgements which are justified in terms of a named source outside the self (attributed) and those which are not so justified, in which case the responsibility for the judgement rests with the speaker/writer. If this were done, self as source and non-attributed would be seen as alternative ways of expressing unsubstantiated judgement, stressing the personal or the impersonal respectively (see Figure 3).

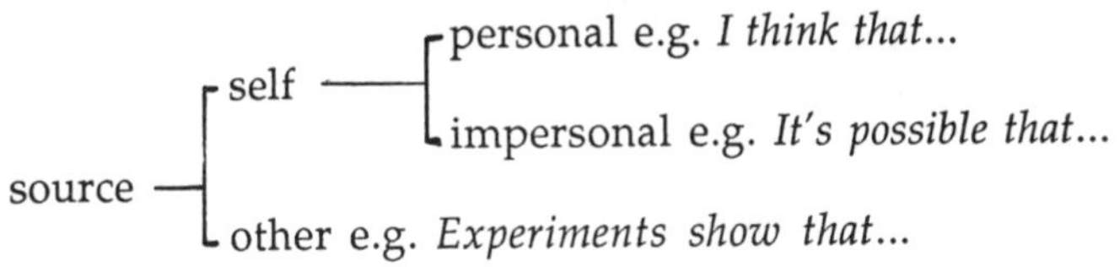

```
                        ┌─ personal e.g. I think that...
              ┌─ self ──┤
              │         └─ impersonal e.g. It's possible that...
   source ────┤
              └─ other e.g. Experiments show that...
```

Figure 3: Alternative general source network

Some support for this alternative may be found in the 'Any Questions' texts, where some statements are modified both by self as source and by non-attributed (see example 12)

> Example 12
> *I think it's possibly true to say that the life of every single female individual living in these islands has got worse in the last ten years (Th2.15)*

Using Figure 3, then, we can legitimately ask how the registers express judgements that are not attributed to an outside source. Table 1 shows a preference for non-attribution over self in *LiS* and a preference for self over non-attribution in *AQ*. These results can then be interpreted within the framework of the degree of value accorded personal opinion as discussed above.

The attributed sources : Figure 2 and Table 2

Another fruitful area of investigation is that of the attributed sources. In these clause complexes, a person or entity other than the writer/speaker is given apparent responsibility for the truth of the proposition, as modified by the report verb. People or entities are therefore used either as evidence for the writer/speaker's judgement, or as evidence that certain judgements, with which the writer/speaker may disagree, are held by others. It is crucial to the study of register to examine what kind of people and entities may play this role because such an examination will tell us what classes of people and things are deemed by a particular sub-culture to be responsible for judgements.

In the *AQ* texts, the **people** fall into three categories. There are specific, named people: *the French Finance Minister; John Major;* the other speakers on the panel, whose words are cited and acknowledged when the current speaker expresses agreement. There are vague sources: *everybody* and *nobody*. In addition, there are groups identified as possessors of certain experiences, such as *no-one that goes round hospitals regularly* or *anybody who regularly travels through London or through any of the big cities*. The **entities** which occur as source are without exception political events, such as *events in the Soviet Union; or Mrs Thatcher's Prime Ministership* .

We may generalise from this to say that the world of 'Any Questions' is a political one, consisting of politicians, the electorate and political-defined events. This is unremarkable in discussions which are, after all, about politics. What is particularly interesting, however, is that some of the most contentious opinions expressed are ascribed to the groups of 'informed general public', quoted above, which exist solely as the construction of the speakers. A good illustration of this is Example 13, in which an informed general public is used to oppose government figures.

> Example 13
> but *no-one that knows that goes round hospitals regularly can believe the figures that the government trots out about investment in the health service are true.*

In other words, the political world is observed and judged by imaginary ordinary people, possessing superior knowledge and experience Given that the audience to the programme consists of such 'ordinary people', a motivation for this is not far to seek, but it is worth noting that this is one of the ways in which speakers construct, and acknowledge the face of, their audiences.

In the *LiS* texts, the **people** are either a named set of researchers in the field, such as *Greif and Gleason*, or a non-specific set of people identified in terms of their academic specialisation, such as *Sociolinguists and other social scientists*. People are also cited non-specifically through references to unspecified texts within the field, such as *studies*, or the interpretation of such texts, such as *evidence*. In short, the people are the doers of experiments and thinkers (cf Myers' 1990 biologists). As regards **entities**, a major distinguishing features of the Lis texts is the high incidence of 'internal' sources of judgement. 'Internal' sources may be glossed as those which do not exist in the world of the reader, as perceived by the writer, prior to the construction of the current text. They consist mainly of references to the experiment being reported as a whole, and to parts of the experiment, such as the results (see example 10), operations performed on the data (see example 14) or summaries of facts concerned with the experiment (see example 15).

Example 14
A chi-square test revealed that this difference in frequency of FN usage was significant (equ). (PRE55)

Example 15
The almost exclusive use of imperatives as the syntactically based directive variant of choice in the current study is not meant to imply that the participants in the migrant subculture have a limited or restricted linguistic repertoire. (DUM27)

The predominance of *other researchers* and *internal entities* as source is consequent upon three features of the register. First, a self-sustaining argument is being constructed, hence the large proportion of *internal* sources. Secondly, it is made to appear, again by the use of internal sources, that experiments and reports of experiments generate their own truth, without the writer being involved in the interpretative process. Thirdly, the process of knowledge construction is intertextual. The claims of the writer are valid only in the light of claims made by other researchers, hence the large number of other researchers as source.

Source choice and culture in two selected texts

In this part of the paper I shall restrict my comments to one example from each of the registers under discussion: the *AQ* text *Thatcher* and the *LiS* text *The spontaneous use of thank you by preschoolers as a function of sex, socioeconomic status, and listener status (SUTY)*. What I shall present is an exploratory discussion of the apparent meanings in each text of particular source choices.

My argument is that the choice of source interacts with both the type of proposition being expressed and the speaker/writer's construction of audience in a way that is unique to each register. Ultimately, it should be possible to posit 'rules' for source choice in each register. My attempts to do so have so far been hindered by the apparent necessity to make unproven assumptions about writer/speaker motivation. I shall confine myself, therefore, to proposing the apparent parameters of variation for each text and to suggesting how these parameters themselves reveal something of the sub-culture of each register.

For the purposes of illustration I shall refer to nine examples which between them represent all instances of projection in the two texts. These are:

SUTY 1
Researchers have noted that lower class, black families tend to emphasise different pragmatic skills...

SUTY 2
Eisenberg concluded that children had formed a category of polite expressions.

SUTY 3
The analysis revealed that girls were more likely to respond.

SUTY 4
It may be that, in novel situations, children attend to the unfamiliar aspects of the situation.

Th1
I think the one woman she did have until she kicked her out was Baroness Young.

Th2
but no-one that knows that goes round hospitals regularly can believe the figures that the government trots out about investment in the health service are true.

Th3
I think I'd probably argue that life became qualitatively worse during the Thatcherite era.

Th4
she had..the ability to extend her hand to other able women and it's quite notable that she didn't do so

Th5
I must say in all honesty that Mrs Thatcher's prime ministership laid to rest for ever the argument that women couldn't take decisions

Two questions constitute the parameters determining source variation in SUTY: *What is the status of the proposition?* and *Is the writer* reporting *or* making *a knowledge claim?* As an example, consider SUTY 3. Here the status of the proposition is a generalisation drawn from numerical data - what I shall call, for convenience, a result. The writer is making a knowledge claim. The source chosen is an entity internal to the text.

In SUTY, three categories of proposition co-occur with projections: generalisations from a range of experiments which are in the process of becoming received knowledge (SUTY 1), results or conclusions from specific experiments (SUTY 2, 3, unknown items which have not yet been researched (SUTY 4). Of the examples, SUTY 3 and 4 are claims by the writer, the other two examples are reports. Below is illustrated the classification of examples:

	writer claim	writer report
generalisation		SUTY 1 *non-sp person*
result	SUTY 3 *internal*	SUTY 2 *sp person*
unknown	SUTY 4 *non-attr*	

Classification of Source Choice in SUTY

The items for which judgement is thus attributed to a source are notably those - generalisations, results and unknowns - which play a large part in the construction of knowledge (Latour and Woolgar 1979). It would appear, then, that the precise choice of source is an integral part of this process of knowledge construction and reflects the academic community's attitude towards how it is done.

In *Thatcher*, the question concerning proposition status is somewhat more complex, in that it appears to be more open to negotiation between speaker and hearers. Broadly speaking, the propositions modified by projections in *Thatcher* may be divided into those that are known to the community, such as TH1, those which are unknowable and essentially contestable (Gallie's term), such as Th3, and those which fall somewhere in the middle, such as Th4 and Th5. In this middle ground of generalisations and extrapolations, there is opportunity for disagreement, not only about propositions, but about whether a proposition is knowable fact or unknowable opinion. What is also noticeable is that, unlike in SUTY, where the community within which the propositions have their status is treated as a single entity, knowledge in *Thatcher* is held differentially. Th1, for example, may be glossed as *The truth of this proposition is known to many members of the community, but not to me.* Th2, on the other hand, may be glossed as *I hold it to be a fact that the government's figures are not true, but this is not generally known by the community.* The first of these may be termed 'unmarked' and the second 'marked', reflecting the fact that the speaker does more interactional work in the second example. The proposition is a surprising, contentious one, whereas the proposition concerning Baronness Young is uncontroversial. In the marked example, the source provides evidence for the building of a consensus. Another example of a marked projection is Th5, where what is contentious about the proposition is that it is in favour of Mrs. Thatcher. It is as if the speaker apologises for holding such as opinion. I am suggesting, then, that the questions which determine the parameters of source choice in *Thatcher* are: What is the status of the proposition? and How much consensus within the community is assumed? The classification of the examples and the source choices is given below:

	marked	unmarked
contestable		Th3
		self
known	Th2	Th1
	person	self
middle	Th5	Th4
	self+say	non-attr

Classification of Source Choice in Thatcher

To summarise the differences between the two texts: In SUTY, everything is treated as ultimately knowable. There are sharp distinctions between the status categories. In *Thatcher*, however, what is talked about is vaguer in terms of knowability. Many items are always contestable, but many others occupy a middle ground between fact and opinion.

A second major difference between the texts is the way that the community is perceived, or constructed, particularly with respect to disagreement. It must be remembered that in SUTY, the writers are contradicting the implications of existing work in the field. The contradiction is carried out using three different source choices: other people's research is attributed to them, a means of simultaneously giving credit and removing writer commitment; the writers' own knowledge claims are attributed to neutral experimental evidence; contradictions are dealt with by reference to areas as yet unresearched. This is very reminiscent of the 'Truth Will Out Device' noted by Gilbert and Mulkay (1984). Despite disagreement, the community remains basically unfragmented. In *Thatcher*, however, it is assumed that the community will always remain fragmented in terms of its access to knowledge and indeed its judgements of what counts as knowledge. Compared to these issues, the matter of expressing an opinion is relatively uncontentious.

Conclusion

The most general conclusion to be drawn from this study is that the expression of modality is best considered as part of a unified concept of evaluation. With regard to register, it is apparent that the two registers in this study are differentiated by how they choose to express modality. When the source of the modality is indicated, as in projecting clauses, they differ in the possible and preferred range of choices.

Conclusions can be drawn also about the sub-cultures of the two registers from the factors determining their choice of source. The extent to which the individual is held responsible for the construction of the world in discourse, for example, is observable by comparing the number of occurrences of *self* as source in each register. Although it has not been possible to establish rules of source choice in individual texts, it appears that the dominant parameters of choice concern the construction of knowledge and the construction of the community. As these constructions differ between communities, so the expression of modality through projecting clauses differs also.

References

Butler, C.S. (1990) Qualifications in science: modal meanings in scientific texts in W.Nash (ed) *The Writing Scholar: Studies in academic discourse* Beverley Hills: Sage, 137-170.

Coates, J (1988) Gossip revisited: language in all-female groups, in Coates and Cameron (eds), *Women in Their Speech Communities: New perspectives on language and sex* London: Longman.

Gilbert, G.N. and M. Mulkay (1984) *Opening Pandora's Box* Cambridge: Cambridge University Press.

Halliday, M.A.K. (1985) *An Introduction to Functional Grammar* London: Arnold.

Hesse, M (1974) *The Structure of Scientific Inference* London: Macmillan.

Holmes, J (1982) Expressing doubt and certainty in English. *RELC Journal* 13, 9-28.

Hunston, S (forthcoming) Evaluation and Ideology in Scientific Discourse, in M. Ghadessy (ed), *Register Analysis: Theory and Practice* London: Pinter.

----(1989), *Evaluation in Experimental Research Articles,* unpublished PhD thesis, University of Birmingham.

----(1991) Interpersonal metaphor: modality in academic and non-academic registers ms, University of Surrey.

Latour, B and Woolgar, S (1979) *Laboratory Life: The social construction of scientific facts* Beverley Hills: Sage.

Makaya, P and Bloor, T (1987) Playing safe with predictions: hedging, attribution and conditions in economic forecasting, in Bloor and Norrish (eds) *Written Language.* London: CILT.

Myers, G (1989) The pragmatics of politeness in scientific articles. *Applied Linguistics* 10, 1-35.

----(1990) *Writing biology: Texts in the social construction of scientific knowledge* Madison: University of Wisconsin Press.

Pinch, T. (1985) Towards an analysis of scientific observation: the externality and evidential significance of observational reports in physics. *Social Studies of Science* 15, 3-36.

Prince, EF, Frader, J and Bosk, C, (1982) On hedging in the physician-physician Discourse', in RJ di Piero (ed), *Linguistics and the Professions* New Jersey: Ablex.

Stubbs, M (1986) A matter of prolonged fieldwork: notes towards a modal grammar of English'. *Applied Linguistics* 7, 1-25.

Thompson, G and Ye, Y (1991) Evaluation in the reporting verbs used in academic papers. *Applied Linguistics* 12, 365-382

Texts cited

Becker and Smenner (1986), The Spontaneous Use of *thank you* by Preschoolers as a Function of Sex, Socioeconomic Status and Listener Status *Language In Society* 15, 537-546 **SUTY**

Dubois (1987), Something on the Order of Around Forty to Forty-Four: Imprecise numerical expressions in bio-medical slide talks *Language In Society* 16, 527-541 **FFF**

Murphy (1988) Personal Reference in English, *Language In Society* 17, 317-349 **PRE**

Weigel and Weigel (1985), Directive Use in a Migrant Agricultural Community: A test of Ervin-Tripp's hypothesis, *Language In Society* 14, 63-80 **DUM**

White (1989), Backchannels Across Cultures: A study of Americans and Japanese, *Language In Society* 18, 59-76 **BAC**

Single Currency *Any Questions* 15.12.90 **SC**
Gorbachev *Any Questions* 21.12.90 **G**
Thatcher *Any Questions* **Th**
Homelessness in Westminster *Any Questions* **HW**
Major and Europe *Any Questions* 6.91 **ME**

Developing Practices of Resistance: Critical reading for students of politics

Romy J. Clark, Institute for English Language Education, University of Lancaster

Introduction

The focus in most recent published EFL and EAP materials for the teaching of reading is on 'filling in the informational gap' by activating the reader's previous knowledge of the topic and genre conventions. This focus can be summed up by the term *background knowledge* (BGK). In this paper I will briefly discuss what I see as the limitations of dominant notions of BGK – as neutral information and objective knowledge. I argue that the notion of BGK should be broadened to include awareness of the social processes of production and interpretation of text, as in the model suggested by Fairclough (1989:25). I will then describe my attempts to develop a more critical framework for Reading for Academic Purposes. This framework is based on a Critical Language Awareness approach (Clark et al, 1987) and rests on the recognition that reading – like writing – is a *social practice*. I end the paper with a brief description of how I use this framework with students (native and non-native speakers of English) of Politics and International Relations at the University of Lancaster.

Background Knowledge

The work in psychology which highlighted the importance of BGK in the successful decoding of texts (for example, Goodman, 1967) obviously made a very positive contribution to the teaching of reading in the late 1960s onwards. Pre-reading techniques, intended to activate what learner readers know already about the reading topic, proliferated in textbooks and classrooms. Later, with the increasing interest in ESP, knowledge of the text type and discourse structure (and much later specific genre analysis)

Graddol, D , L. Thompson
and M. Byram (eds) (1993)
Language and Culture, Clevedon:
BAAL and Multilingual Matters

also became important. The idea was that explicit reference to the reader's BGK (including cultural schemata and generic structure) would facilitate understanding of the text. Anticipation and prediction exercises were developed to facilitate this kind of conscious drawing on BGK. Any gaps in 'knowledge' could be plugged by pre-reading discussion, etc. These approaches are useful in as far as they go but I believe they leave out crucial dimensions because, wittingly or not, most of the work in this tradition treats the writer, the reader and the text asocially and still privileges the 'single meaninged text'. There is no place for polysemy. The contribution of BGK is seen, I believe, as making the understanding by the reader of the writer's meaning more accessible – or to help the reader read the text 'accurately' and not misread because of faulty schema or lack of knowledge about the writer's world. There seems to be no real room for alternative competing schemata (views of what is appropriate, etc) because the assumption seems to be that there is only one set of appropriate schemata for this particular culture. The notion of struggle over meaning is totally lacking in this tradition except in the sense that it is hard work to work out the meaning of a text.

Let me give a few examples to illustrate what I mean:

> From Nuttall 1982:6-7: *the reader and the writer should have certain things in common, if communication between them is to take place. The minimum requirement is that they should share the same code; that they should write and understand the same language.* A more interesting requirement she points to is that the writer and reader should share certain *assumptions about the world* and the way it works. She says: *We saw that if the writer expects his* (sic) *reader to have a basic understanding of chemistry, the text will not be readily understood by anyone who lacks this.* She goes on to refer to problems of mismatch between the presuppositions of the writer and those of the reader. This last comment seems even more promising but the follow-up is disappointing. Nuttall goes on to give a list of examples (pp 7-9), and it soon becomes clear that what she means by presupposition is only what the writer expects the reader to know in terms of factual knowledge.

> Anderson and Pearson in Carrell, Devine and Eskey, 1988:42 :*A schema is an abstract knowledge structure.* They go on to give the example of *the typical person's knowledge of ship christening.* Again, however, there is an assumption that there is only one appropriate schema for ship's christenings – just neutral 'facts' about who does what and how – no alternative or resistant schema envisages, only 'defective' ones. The Campaign for Nuclear Disarmament certainly offered a radical alternative to the naming ceremony of the Trident Submarine in Barrow-in-Furness in April 1992 by, for example, wearing black armbands and organising

alternative names for the submarine and a die-in to coincide, at the yard, with the official ceremony. We can all think of other situations in which competing schemata are more readily imaginable: eg., the classroom lesson and the accompanying roles and behaviours of teacher and pupils; what constitutes appropriate foreign policy behaviour; and how a diplomat should conduct negotiations. Apart from anything else, it seems hard to see how change in society occurs and how views of what is appropriate shift without a notion of struggle between opposing views.

From Carrell and Eisterhold, in Carrell, Devine and Eskey (1988: 82-3): *reading comprehension depends crucially on the reader's being able to relate information from the text to already existing background information we must be particularly sensitive to reading problems that result from the implicit cultural knowledge presupposed by a text.* The example they then give is about transportation in the US and the difficulties readers had in understanding the *specific schema of the cars/mass transportation opposition*: back to 'factual' knowledge again. A little later they quote the example of a Muslim student who 'refused to even consider the premise of' the sentence *Because we can't be free of prejudice in the area of religion, we should not practice a religion.* It seems to me that an excellent opportunity is missed here, namely to explore with students *why* they resist sharing the meaning a writer is trying to put across and therefore raise the readers' awareness of how important the socio-political identity of the writer and the reader is. An opportunity for the students to learn how to challenge the writer and say why. The rather dismissive comment *the student even refused to consider the premise* shows shocking insensitivity, in my view, but above all reveals the naivety of the view of reading and the reader-text-writer relationship.

Under the heading 'classroom activities' (p.85) they say the following: Since no author can compensate for the individual variation among readers, especially readers from different cultural backgrounds, this is one of the roles of the teacher in the ESl/EFL reading classroom. As teachers, we can approach this problem by manipulating either one of two variables: the text and/or the reader. Apart from the problems I have with the notion of 'manipulating the reader', they use the expression 'previewing' for preparatory exercises for difficult texts: the problem is how can the teacher predict what difficulties the individual readers are going to have and why. It seems to me that there is another problem with their position. Differences between different readers should not be swept away or treated as a 'problem'. Rather, they should be treated as a resource – exploiting the differences to illustrate concretely how different readings are not only possible but inevitable. Secondly, it is important to explore how resistance to a writer's meaning may make the reading more difficult, until the reader actually realizes that that is what is happening, rather than him/her just not being able to understand the text, in the conventional sense. This can actually be very liberating and motivating for students.

Alderson and Urquhart (1984:xviii-ix) point out, *the tradition of research into (reading) 'skills' is based upon the assumption that texts have predictable meanings, which can be extracted if only the reader is skilful.* Widdowson (1979) suggests that text have have 'potential for meaning' but unfortunately the pedagogical take up of these significant insights, namely that texts are only made meaningful by actual readers who will vary in their readings, is, in my view, disappointing. Widdowson, for example, stresses that the differences in meaning between readers depend crucially on purpose and knowledge. The Alderson and Urquhart edited collection of papers also seems to concentrate on 'deficient' reader strategies rather than on the social dimensions of reading and the struggle over meaning. The main focus then is on *information* and *knowledge* which the student needs in order to 'read' the text successfully, ie as the writer intended it. Culture is included only as one form of information or knowledge that the reader needs in order to plug into the writer's meaning.

With respect to the problems my students have with understanding and/or accepting Western cultural and political schemata and being constructed as poor readers (or simply 'wrong') when they disagree or cannot understand why they disagree or cannot articulate their reasons, there is little in this literature to help me and them. In terms of BGK in the conventional sense of course I can help them find ways to plug the gaps in their knowledge of the particular concept/event or whatever but it seems to me that I need to help them go further than that. They need to identify the socio-political reasons behind the thinking, the implications of the thinking and how this relates to their own experience or worldview. They also need to work out whether they want to accommodate to this thinking and be constructed in the same line of thinking or whether they wish to resist such a construction of themselves as compliant reading subjects. Part of this is recognizing and being able to deconstruct, for example, ethnocentric discourse and the ideological presuppositions that make the text cohere (Hall, 1982), which of course are often difficult for any of us to do. his is precisely why they are so successful. Students need to examine the implications of being constructed as a poor reader because of not sharing the implicit worldview expressed in most of the textbooks and articles they have to read (ie US-dominated, Western viewpoints). Ethnocentrism and its accompanying world view is hard for the students to resist also because of the dominance of these views in Politics and International Relations outside the Western centre –

which may well be why they have been sent here to study in the first place, of course! They also recognize that they are constructed for the most part as junior members of the academic discourse community and are therefore powerless to challenge those in authority – be they established writers or the lecturers who tell them to read the books. What they certainly do not need in my view is a 'Study Skills teacher' practising assimilationist policies by teaching them how to better conform to the dominant Western political culture. Hence my concerns with critical reading, understanding the underpinnings of that culture and developing practices of resistance – for those who want them.

So, to sum up so far, although the view of the reader as an active partner is a significant shift away from old notions of reading as one of the passive skills (along with listening!), there are still, to my mind, a number of problems and limitations with the current view in many EAP materials. These concern crucially the reader-writer-text relationship in the wider social context. There is an alternative view which I shall now describe.

CLA and reading as a social practice

I believe that it is important for readers in general, and my students in particular, to understand the social practices in which reading and writing are embedded rather than to attempt to acquire skills as if they were neutral technologies, equally available to everyone and independent of meaning (Street in Stubbs: 1986:7). You read differently when you agree, when you subconsciously disagree and when you consciously disagree (cf the three decoding positions described by Hall, 1980). And by learning how to recognize your own beliefs and standpoints and cultural values you learn to treat reading as a social practice rather than just as a skill. Below I outline briefly my own classroom practice.

The framework: Critical Language Awareness

For reasons of space I will not rehearse what CLA is but refer readers to descriptions elsewhere (Clark et al.,1990, 1991; Fairclough, 1989; Ivanic, 1988). However, I include below a list of some key concepts missing from the general view of BGK in EAP materials:

Reading as a social practice: readers, writers and texts as socially shaped and shaping

Ideological presupposition. In my view this is the key concept. Hall (1982) defines ideological presupposition as the entailed set of linked unstated propositions based on ideological premises. He gives as an example: *a statement like 'the strike of Leyland toolmakers today further weakened Britain's economic position' was premised on a whole set of taken-for-granted propositions about how the economy worked, what the national interest was and so on. For it to win credibility, the whole logic of capitalistic production had to be assumed to be true* (1982:74)

Intertextuality: a complex notion, but briefly – texts draw on other specific texts, discourses or genres and adopt varying relationships towards them – agreement, opposition, etc; readers use the intertextual cues within the text (eg, direct respresentations such as quotations, reported speech; the discourse of commerce used in a text about education; the narrative form of the 'Boys Own Adventure Story' in reports on the Gulf War) to interpret the text and draw on their knowledge of other texts, discourses and genres to interpret the specific text (See Belsey,1980; Fairclough, 1989)

Polysemy: the text as multimeaninged, struggle over meaning, texts as arenas of struggle (See Volosinov, 1973; Fiske, 1987)

Modality: that part of the grammar which indicates the truthfulness, reliability or authoritativeness of an utterance. Modality shows a version of reality as the speaker/writer sees it or intends it to be be seen by the hearer/reader. (See Fowler et al, 1979:200)

Reader positioning: how the writer-text attempt to persuade the reader to take on a particular reading position. The pronouns used can be very revealing of this. For example, the use of 'we' can be used to set up a relationship of complicity between the writer's position and the reader's by assuming sharedness of viewpoint. (See Fairclough, 1989)

Decoding positions: this refers to Hall's useful 'three hypothetical positions' for decoding (1980:136 ff) : (i) The dominant hegemonic position in which the reader is within the writer's reference code and accepts it. (ii) The negotiated code in which The reader is within the writer's code but contests its appropriacy in this particular instance for his/her reading. (iii) The oppositional position in which the reader is totally outside the writer's code

Awareness must come from working with real language interaction – not contrived examples. Awareness work should be purposeful, ie. in my case Students work on real texts, mainly those they have to read for their main course and which they really need to understand and have views on. They do not do separate 'reading practice' for me other than some initial training which I describe below.

Critical Reading for students in Politics and International Relations

The students form a multicultural group – many from so-called Third World, together with students from the UK and other parts of Europe, the US and Canada. They are diplomats, military, interpreters, etc – mostly mature people with lots of experience who are studying for an MA in Diplomacy/International Relations/Defence Studies or a Diploma in International Relations. The very nature of the group provides an excellent opportunity for exploring real different reading positions and some possible reasons for them.

In the first term we focus on academic writing, viewed and analysed as a social practice. We spend quite a bit of time on Critical Language Awareness and this serves as a useful backdrop to the work on reading as a social practice in the second term. The work on writing is important because the students have already become more aware of the nature of discourse and text as socially constructed and constructing and of themselves as socially constructed student subjects (see Clark et al, 1989, for a description of this work)

In our work on reading we begin with the students discussing in small groups the following statement, what it means to them and what the implications are: 'Reading is a social practice'. The whole class then shares views and we make a record of the ideas that come up – including my own.

The next step is to turn these perceptions and practical experiences into a handout which attempts to systematise them and acts as both a training aid and a checklist of things to do when reading. The latest version of this handout is given in the Appendix. It incorporates the key concepts mentioned above. I point out that the suggested 'steps' are only discrete for analytical purposes to ease discussion but not in actual reading practice. In subsequent sessions we apply the analysis in practice to a range of texts, using the Handout as a reminder of things to look for.

First of all we analyse a range of newspaper articles. In 1991 we focused (at the students' request) on The Gulf War. I use newspaper texts for two main reasons. Firstly, it is often easier to see what is going on in such a text – the features are more exaggerated. Secondly it encourages students to read a range of newspapers so that they have an idea of the range of opinions circulating on contemporary issues

Subsequently, we analyse texts which they have to read as part of their own studies. So far we have read parts of A.J.P Taylor's *Origins of the Second World War*; A book on Northern Ireland; and a book on Dependency Theory.

The basic classroom procedure is as follows: we make notes individually on our thoughts about the text, author, topic, purpose, attitudes, etc. (see 'pre-reading' on the handout) before we start reading the whole text. Sometimes we discuss any points the students want to raise at this stage. This might include, for example, sharing information and views about the author and working out what 'decoding position' we are each starting off in. We then read all or part of the text (depending on the length some texts are read over more than one session) and highlight bits we find significant in terms of a critical reading. We then discuss our different readings of the text and try to justify our readings to the group by referring to the features we found significant and the reasons for our interpretations and any shifts in 'decoding position' and why.

Appendix

Critical Reading: A Suggested Approach
You can try and apply the following 'steps' to any text. They may not all be relevant to all texts, but the general approach may help you to ream more critically.

BEFORE READING THE TEXT:
ask yourself the following questions:
• why am I reading this? What is my purpose? Why is it on my reading list?
• what do I know about the author, the publisher, the circumstances of publication and the type of text? How do these affect my attitude towards and expectations of what I am about to read? Why?
• what are my own views of the event(s) or topic before I start reading this particular text?
• what other texts (written and spoken) on this or similar topics am I familiar with? What are my views about them?

WHILE READING THE TEXT:
• while reading the text highlight the verbs and any modifiers:

- ask yourself what the unmodified verbs tell you about the 'truth' value of what the author is saying and how this affects your readingand what the modified verbs tell you - what is the effect of the modification?
- look at any passivizations and see if you can reconstruct the agent: ask yourself what the effect on you as a reader is of
  a)passives for which you can find the agent and
  b)passives for which you cannot
- highlight significant (to you) instances of nominalizations and see if you can reconstruct participants and processes:
- ask yourself what the effect on you as a reader is
  a)if you can and
  b)if you cannot
- look at the verbs of reporting (events and other people's ideas): ask ask yourself what the selected verbs tell you about the 'truth' value of what the author is telling you and what your reaction is what is the effect on you of
  a)attribution? and
  b)non-attribution?
- look at the way the writer uses quotations, summaries, citations and paraphrase: how do these referencing practices affect your attitudes to the text? Is there any 'slippage' of voice from attributed to author voice? How does this affect the authoritativeness of the text?
- consider what other texts and genres and what discourses this text is drawing on: how does this affect your reading of the text? Why?
- examine the author's argumentation: highlight any evidence the author supplies for his/her arguments:
  is there enough evidence? is it convincing? can you think of counter evidence or counter examples? how do your answers affect your reading of the text?
  does the author make his/her premises explicit or not? Do you agree with them or not. So what is the effect on you as a reader?
- look at the way the writer uses personal pronouns like 'you' and 'we' how does this position the reader? Do you accept that positioning? Why or why not?
- examine the choice of words the author makes, especially nouns, adjectives and lexical verbs:
- what do they tell you about the author's attitude to his/her message? and to the reader? Do you accept these wordchoices? Why or why not?
- look at the author's choice of metaphors:
- what do they tell you about the author'as attitude towards his/her message and the reader? What is your reaction? Why?
- what are the idelogical presuppositions behind the text? do you share them? if so, what is the effect on you as a reader?

AFTER READING
Ask yourself the following questions:
- have I fulfilled my purpose(s) for reading? if not, what will I do next?
- have my views of the event(s) or topic been reinforced or altered in any way? How? Where do I now stand?
- what have I learned? what do I feel? How can I use this reading experience, now and in the future?

References

Alderson, J. C. and Urquhart A. H. (1984) *Reading in a Foreign Language* London:Longman

Belsey, C. (1980) *Critical Practice* London:Routledge

Carrell, P., Devine J. and Eskey D. (1988) *Interactive Approaches to Second Language Reading* Cambridge: Cambridge University Press.

Clark, R., Cottey, A., Constantinou C. and Yeoh, O.C. (1990) *Rights and Obligations in Student Writing* in Clark et al (eds) *Language and Power, Selected Proceedings of the BAAL Annual Meeting, Lancaster 15-17 Sept. 1989*, London: CILT

Clark, R. Fairclough, N., Ivanic, R. and Martin-Jones, M. (1990) Critical Language Awareness I, *Language and Education*, vol 4,4 1990; vol 5,1, 1991, Multilingual Matters

Clark, R. and Ivanic R (1991) *Consciousness-raising about the Writing Process* in P. Garrett and C. James (eds) *Language Awareness in the Classroom* London: Longman

Currie, P. and Cray, E. (1987) *Strictly Academic*

Fairclough, N.L. (1989) *Language and Power* London: Longman

Fiske, J. (1987) *Television Culture* London:Routledge

Fowler, R. R., Hodge, G., Kress and Trew, T. (1979) *Language and Control* London: RKP

Goodman, K. (1967) Reading as a Psycholinguistic Guessing Game in: *Journal of the Reading Specialist*, 126-135

Hall, S. (1982) The rediscovery of 'idealogy': return of the repressed in media studies, in: Gurevitch et al (eds) *Culture, Society and the Media* London: Methuen

Hall, S. (1980) Encoding/decoding in: Hall et al (eds) *Culture, Media, Language*, London:Hutchinson

Ivanic, R. (1988) Critical Language Awareness in Action in *Language Issues* 2.2. pp. 2-7

Nuttall, C. (1982) *Teaching Reading Skills in a Foreign Language* London:Heinemann

Sanka, A.L. (1981) *Skilful Reading* Prentice Hall

Smith, M. and S. (1990) *A Study Skills Handbook* Oxford: Oxford University Press.

Stubbs, M. (1986) *Educational Linguistics* Oxford: Blackwell

Sullivan, T. (1979) *Reading and Understanding* London: National Extension College

Thompson, J.B. (1984) *Studies in the Theory of Ideology* Cambridge: Polity Press

Tomlinson, B. and Ellis, R. (1988) *Reading Advanced* Oxford: Oxford University Press.

Volosinov, V.N. (1973) *Marxism and the Philosophy of Language* New York:Seminar Press

Wallace, M. (1980) *Study Skills in English* Cambridge: Cambridge University Press.

Widdowson, H.G. (1979) *Explorations in Applied Linguistics* Oxford: Oxford University Press.

Song-Lashing as a Communicative Strategy in Interpersonal Conflicts in Yoruba Land: a sociolinguistic appraisal

Tope Omoniyi, University of Reading

Introduction

In traditional Yoruba society, songs serve a variety of communicative purposes: for funeral consolations through dirges; for expanding mythological themes; for rituals; for inspiring warriors; for folkloric entertainment and for launching verbal assaults in inter-personal conflicts. In this study we attempt a sociolinguistic appraisal of the music of assault.

Most of the earlier research on 'conflict talk' has been carried out within a framework of either discourse analysis or theories of pragmatics. The preoccupation in such studies has been with analysing or describing the structure of conflict talk and the roles played by participants in the exchange process. There is thus, a greater concentration on conflict talk which takes the form of straight verbal exchanges or disputes between aggrieved or disagreeing parties and a corresponding neglect of songs as a communicative strategy in conflict situations. The competence of participants in these verbal exchanges is measured in terms of the size of their repertoire of logical arguments and the abuse words or phrases. There is limited research in the sociolinguistics of conflict talk (eg Stross (1975), Salamone (1976) Heath (1983) Katriel (1985) Eder (1990)).

This paper will attempt a sociolinguistic analysis of a specific mode of conflict discourse, 'song-lashing', which is a popular strategy used by participants in conflict situations in traditional Yoruba society in Nigeria. This study is closely linked to Stross's (1975) analysis of linguistic creativity in Tzeltal songs. Stross makes a distinction between standard songs and improvised songs. Standard songs, he says, are those that contain obligatory invariant phrases, while the improvised ones are those that vary from one individual and context to another, both in melodic pattern and in content. Yoruba song-lashing involves two

Graddol, D , L. Thompson
and M. Byram (eds) (1993)
Language and Culture, Clevedon:
BAAL and Multilingual Matters

varieties of songs: proverbial songs (orin-owe) and abuse songs (orin-eebu). The proverbial songs fit into Stross's category of Standard songs. They are largely invariant and contain established metaphors, proverbs, and other figures of speech. In the main they attack individuals' violation of societal norms and values. The abuse songs on the other hand may or may not retain a general melodic pattern, but definitely vary in content depending on the target of the attack. Generally, abuse songs are easier to interpret than the proverbial ones. Abuse songs are similar to Labov's (1990) 'derogatory labelling' which she says is a device for identity negotiation. However, some songs are 'hybrids' incorporating elements from both types. The conflicts in which they are used are ritual in nature, since they are not intended to result in a resolution. There are also Yoruba conflict songs which are aimed at resolving disputes (cf. Stross's observations on the Tzeltal), but this will not be our concern here. Since song-lashing is used more frequently by females than by males, the participants will be referred to as 'she' throughout this paper.

Songs of assault are, ironically, usually entertaining. There is almost always audience participation - cheering, laughing and savouring the exchanges, until the conflict intensifies into a brawl when they become either arbitrators or spectators. Some of the songs contain humour and taboo words, particularly if the intention is to ridicule or mock the target individual. On the other hand, in a very tense situation, such light-hearted mockery gives way to highly offensive insults or even curses. A participant's competence in the usage of this mode is judged by her ability to select the appropriate song for the occasion, and for the intended target. Success is judged in terms of the impact on the opponent in what Salamone (1976) calls symbolic warfare.

Socio-cultural setting

The Yoruba are the third largest ethnic group in Nigeria after the Hausa and Igbo, according to 1979 government census estimates. They occupy the south-west section of the country. In rural society, a clear distinction is made between 'traditional wisdom' and 'academic wisdom'. A competent member of that society is expected to know the behavioural norms of the society, and to respond appropriately to utterances or songs, particularly in conflict situations. One who fails to demonstrate such competence is derogatorily termed 'omo lo'le lo gb'esi wa' (that is, 'a child who goes home to fetch a response').

In the last half-century geographical mobility has been so extensive that Yoruba traditional culture has been exposed to considerable external influence, particularly through Western education. Urbanisation, in particular, has led to cultural changes in which some traditional practices are shed and other 'alien' or 'modern' traits are acquired. Song-lashing, for example, is a traditional feature of rural life and is not a popular urban cultural trait. In the city, it can be found mainly in urban 'motor-parks' (long-distance coach stations) and artisan workshops, which are serviced by workers who have retained the vestiges of their former rural life-style.

Song-lashing is traditionally rendered in a local dialect which reflects a particular geographical location. This remains the case in even an urban setting such as Lagos, where a higher status dialect of Yoruba is generally spoken. The usual consequence is that the song-lasher is referred to as 'ara oke' or 'ara oko', that is, 'one from the rural interior' or 'one from a farm settlement'. In view of this, even those who have a rich repertoire of traditional conflict songs and are adept at using the strategy, tend not to use them in Lagos. This attempt to avoid the rural stigma may partially and indirectly account for the visibly higher number of 'fist-to-face' encounters in Lagos, where people opt for more direct confrontation than the prolonged process of first indirectly assaulting opponents through songs and only resorting to violence when this process has been exhausted.

Participants and their relationships

Although there are no statistics to support this, observation has shown and other reports in the literature (Salamone, 1976) confirm that song-lashing is more frequently used by women. Its indirectness is interpreted as a portrayal of weakness if used by men.

Conflict situations in which abuse songs are used quite often involve persons belonging to the same peer group. These people could be members of the same or different community organisations engaged in inter-group or intra-group conflict. The point to note here is that there is a conflict of opinion or interests which results in a dispute. The target's interpretation of the songs and her identification of herself as the target would trigger another series of abuse songs in response. In the alternative scenario, particularly where the initial target is not in any doubt as to her physical ability to 'deal with' the 'aggressor', she openly challenges her to stop singing indirectly and cryptically. This could eventually result in a brawl in the absence of intervention by an older person.

These songs are most common among teenagers. It is believed that use diminishes with maturity. However, it is also used by people in their thirties and forties. Apart from peer group conflicts, disputes involving people from different age groups may also involve the use of song-lashing if the people in dispute share a common interest. Polygamous squabbles are an illustration of this. Women married to the same husband may enter into disputes. It is more common for the junior wife to use this strategy to make allegations against or to insult the senior wife rather than vice-versa. This is probably because tradition expects a certain amount of respect to be shown to a senior. However if the junior wife is obviously the husband's favourite and thus has a back-up of greater social power, the senior wife may also use song-lashing. In either case, it is unthinkable that the confrontation should take place in the husband's presence. It is also preferable that there should be no spectator who can report as a witness to the 'arbiter' when he gets home. It is acceptable if the spectator is a friend or relation of the singer (cf. Salamone, 1976:363).

Teenage children of these polygamous homes may also sing abuse or proverbial songs at their stepmothers. Usually, however, it is the children of the senior wife, particularly those born before the junior wife came into the family, who would use these songs. Tradition puts them on a slightly higher point in the family hierarchy and thus forbids the junior wife from passing any disciplinary sanctions on them. If the children of the junior wife misbehave, the senior wife is empowered to call them to order. It is therefore a taboo for these children to sing abuse songs at her.

Husbands rarely use these songs. Their relatively powerful position within the family enables them to summon, challenge and reprimand wife or child. However, a husband could subtly forewarn a wife or child of the possibility of a physical reprimand by singing a proverbial song. Husbands would not use abuse songs on their wives or children under any circumstances. It is also unlikely that people who share a consanguine relationship, such as siblings of the same parents, would use these songs in conducting their disputes. Rather, they would exchange direct verbal insults or even duel. Those who frequently resort to song-lashing tend to be shunned socially.

Situational contexts and appropriateness

Several factors, socio-cultural and functional, may account for the adoption of song-lashing as a strategy in a conflict. For example, in a situation in which the participants are of unequal social power, the weaker may consider song-lashing.Or in conflict situations, when people quite often do not want to be labelled the aggressor, it is not unusual to use song-lashing to lure the other party into hitting first. It may also be used to arouse a sense of guilt and shame. Finally, song-lashing is done to establish the perpetrator of a bad deed. A hypothetical name is used, but the allegations reveal who the intended target is. The 'culprit' or offender may or may not confess.

Respective domains of language use have appropriate variants of a language delineated for them, to depart from these hampers communication. In song-lashing unless a song type is rendered which is appropriate for the conflict situation communication breaks down and the target does not get the intended message. The song is thus ineffective. Similarly, if a song is badly timed, it may fail to communicate because some songs depend on the presence or absence of spectators to achieve effect. Several factors thus combine to determined the appropriateness of songs in a conflict situation.

The theme of the dispute is an important consideration, particularly as this determines the kind of analogies, similes, and metaphors built into the song. They also have to be relevant to the individual or the societal circumstance of the participants in the conflict. In other words, the target should have no scope for misinterpreting the intended meaning. Grimshaw (1990:283) classifies the content of conflict talk into four categories, (a) settling disputed claims between two parties; (b) establishing and negotiating personal identities; (c) performing socialising functions; and (d) indulging in verbal play or sport (the strategy of Turkish boys' verbal duelling rhymes would fit into this category: see Dundes et al., 1972). The songs used in song-lashing belong more or less to Grimshaw's second and third categories.

Apart from theme of dispute and participants, the time of day is equally important. It may, for instance, be counter-productive to start song-lashing first thing in the morning because Yoruba tradition holds that the morning determines the course of the entire day. Hence, it is considered unreasonable to get into a conflict very early in the day. However, in other disputes, particularly polygamous, the timing has less to do with the time of day and more with the absence of the husband, his relations and any other person who might testify against the participants. Any insults reported by the target can therefore be denied before an arbitrator if there are no witnesses. Timing is another dimension of contextual appropriateness.

Let us now consider some illustrations of conflict songs of the two broad types we have identified earlier. All the quoted examples are in the Ibolo dialect of Yoruba. These examples were collected using a mixed methodology: First, observations of song lashing events were made from a spectator's perspective. Second, the observed contexts were discussed with some participants. Third, since disputes are not scheduled this makes it difficult to record songs in context. Conflict songs were therefore recorded out of context for this study.

Example 1 (Abuse song: physical peculiarity)

Ma ro nko yo re 'le	I'll have a container for salt
Ma ro nko yo re 'le o	I'll have a container for salt
B'ota mi se	If my enemy has
B'ota mi se ropba leeke	If my enemy has plastic cheeks
Ma ro nko yo re 'le o	I'll have a container for salt

The singer ridicules the target's chubby cheeks by comparing them to a plastic container.

Example 2 (Abuse song: physical peculiarity)

Wakala wokolo wo bi se nlo	Seehow she's walking,
Ogede gbomo pon b'eti kalasa	The laden banana stalk with extended ear lobes (leaves).
Iya re nmo fi ponmo ete jo	It's your mother I look like
Ponmo ponmo ete bi agbado	with thick lips like maize

This song ridicules the target's style of movement, her humped back and the size of her ears, by metaphoric reference to a banana stalk. The target must previously have ridiculed the present singer for her thick lips: this insult is now turned back on the target and given a greater sting by being extended to her mother. Wakala wokolo on the first line has no real semantic property; it simply describes her clumsy manner of walking. The song can only be rendered if the target is walking past the singer: it would be inappropriate to it in another situation. In comparison to Example 1, this song would more rapidly lead to a brawl.

Example 3 (Hybrid song: physical peculiarity)

Ori mo se mi o	Fate, don't bring me bad luck,
Ori mo se mi	Fate, don't bring me bad luck.
Enia lo se Suweba	Somebody's brought Suweba bad luck.
Ori mo se mi	Fate, don't bring me bad luck

Oloju ede o	She (Suweba) has eyes like a shrimp's,
Oluju ede	She has eyes like a shrimp's.
Emi o to Suweba	I didn't provoke her,
Oloju ede	She has eyes like a shrimp's

This song also ridicules a body part: the eye. The singer likens her subject's eyes to shrimps because of their small size. The name Suweba is fictitious, and the target is expected to recognize that she is the persona in the song from the physical peculiarity mentioned. The song establishes the singer's initial innocence and indirectly ascribes the role of aggressor to the target.

Example 4 (Proverbial song: behaviour)

Inugbo l'obo ngbe	Monkeys live in the forest,
Inugbo l'obo ngbe	Monkeys live in the forest.
Enikan i kole adete sigboro o	No-one builds a leper colony in the city,
Inugbo l'obo ngbe	Monkeys live in the forest.

Songs of this type primarily attack anti-social behaviour. The allegation may not be explicitly mentioned in the songs, but the target is clearly told she does not belong within human society.

Example 5 (Hybrid song: behaviour)

O s'enia s'eranko	It happens with humans and animals alike,
O s'enia s'eranko	It happens with humans and animals alike
Alabosi nf'omore lomu	The nuisance is breast-feeding her baby,
O'senia s'eranko.	It happens with humans and animals alike.

This song establishes that although the target may have some human characteristics, she is actually an animal.

Example 6 (Hybrid song: polygamous dispute)

O de'le nile d'ahoro o	She arrived and the house became choked,
O de'le nile d'ahoro	She arrived and the house became choked,
Iyawo elese pebu	The wife with the shapeless feet,
O de'le nile d'ahoro	She arrived and the house became choked.
K'oto de lati npe baba o	Until she came, we called him 'baba',
Iyawo elete ponmo	The wife with the thick lips,
K'oto de lati npe baba	Until she came, we called him 'baba'.

The first stanza of this song tells the junior wife that she is unwelcome. If a new wife tries to change established family practice, even if her alternative is better the senior wife could attack her initiative out of jealousy, as in the second stanza of the song.

Example 7 (Children's abuse song)

Guguru ta pee	Popcorn pops,
Guguru ta pee	Popcorn pops,
Obo'ya re ta bi agbodo	Your mother's cunt pops like corn,
Guguru ta pee	Popcorn pops.

Abuse songs such as this directly insult the target: whereas other abuse songs refer to her obliquely in the third person, this type uses second person pronouns and adjectives. This category of songs is restricted to pre-pubertal children. It is worth noting that songs which include taboo words referring to the sexual organs are more widely used by boys than by girls. This is in conformity with traditional expectations that girls will be shy and reserved. The boys who use such songs will not do so in the presence of adults (cf. Wolfram's, 1973 report on ritualistic use of language among East Harlem Puerto Ricans).

Example 8 (Abuse song: permanent physical deformity)

Onigbegbe l'orun	Only one with goitre
Lo le s'aya asopa	Can marry one with inflamed testes
O di roto, O di gbenko	
O di roto, O di gbenko	

Songs of this type resemble other abuse songs in that they ridicule the target's physical peculiarity; they are, however, less frequently used. When they are used the intention is to cause great hurt, and the reactions they provoke are often grave. The last two lines of this song make no real sense, except to demonstrate the shape of the goitre and the inflamed testes, and they are usually rendered with clasped fists to the neck and to the groin.

Song-lashing and urban Lagos society

Song-lashing is a communicative strategy employed in conflict situations and is confined to the rural areas. We must add, though, that 'urban' has been conceived of in cultural as well as geographical terms. There are, for instance, those towns and cities which would, considering economic and demographic factors, qualify as urban centres but in which traditional lifestyles are still prevalent. Ibadan, the largest city in West Africa, is one such place. Here, unlike Lagos, song-lashing remains a socio-cultural feature of conflict situations among the people.

It will be recalled that any inhabitant of Lagos who indulges in song-lashing is treated with the disdain considered appropriate to 'rustics'. Ironically, Yoruba popular music (Yo-Pop), which draws heavily on both abuse and proverbial songs for its lyrics, is warmly embraced by the very elites who display such snobbery towards this traditional verbal resource when encountered in its 'raw' form. It is commonplace to find rival Yo-Pop groups launching musical assaults against each other. Urban settlers then employ these recorded songs as ammunition against the other party in a conflict. For example, Ebenezer Obey's 'Ko s'ogbon te le da' ('There's nothing you can do', i.e. there's no pleasing some people) could be played within earshot of a selfish neighbour who would not be satisfied no matter what effort one made to placate them. Followers of the different groups are able to interpret their idols' songs correctly in terms of identifying the intended targets. However, Yo-Pop probably uses more proverbial songs than abuse songs, alluding to folklore, religious faiths and so on.

Also, in the introduction to this paper, we referred to a peripheral urban population who have not been assimilated into the mainstream urban society and therefore still extensively exhibit rural traits. Some of these people make no pretentions to being Lagosians: they first and foremost see themselves as having rural 'roots' and do not hide the fact. They rarely make any effort to speak Lagos Yoruba, and among them song-lashing is a potent weapon in a conflict. This may sound similar to Labov's (1972) observation in his study of Martha's Vineyard. However, these Lagos rural-urban people do not appear to have a politically motivated loyalty to their indigenous communicative traditions such as Labov's subjects demonstrated. In the present case, it appears to be more of a matter of convenience, more so since this adherence to rural traits is more widespread among an older generation who probably are not longer linguistically flexible.

Conclusion

Song-lashing is a communicative strategy which has to be effectively manipulated. The concept of communicative competence applies to the use of this strategy since variations of situation and participants match variations in song selection and composition. The ability of individual participants to discriminate between appropriateness and inappropriateness is a measure of their communicative competence in the language.

Song-lashing is both an urban and a rural phenomenon, but the traditional form is restricted to the rural areas where some people would prefer physical assault to this effective musical assault. It also serves some entertainment function for spectators and when presented in the medium of Yoruba Popular music. Finally, there are also song forms for conflict resolution.

References

Dundes, A., Leach J. and Ozkok B. (1972) The Strategy of Turkish Boys' Verbal Duelling Rhymes. in Gumperz and Hymes pp. 130-60.

Eder, D. (1990) Variations in Adolescent Female Conflict Talk in A. Grimshaw (ed).

Fishman, J. (ed) (1968) *Readings in the Sociology of Language*. The Hague: Mouton.

Grimshaw, A. (ed), *Conflict Talk: Sociolinguistic Investigation of Arguments in Conversations*. Cambridge: Cambridge University Press.

Grimshaw, A.D. (1990) Research in Conflict Talk: envoi and reprise, in Grimshaw, A. (ed).

Gumperz, J. and Hymes, D. (ed.s) (1972) *Directions in Sociolinguistics*. New York: Holt Rinehart and Winston.

Heath, B. (1983) Processes of Dispute Management among Urban Black Children, in *Ways with Words: Language, Life and Work in Communities and Classrooms*. Cambridge: Cambridge University Press.

Katriel, T. (1985) Brogez: Ritual and Strategy in Israeli Children's Conflicts, in *Language in Society*. Vol. 14, no.4, Dec. 1985, pp. 467-90.

Kochran, T. (1981) *Black and White Styles in Conflict*. Chicago: University for Chicago Press.

Labov, T. (1990) Ideological Themes in reports of Racial Conflict, in Grimshaw, A. (ed).

Labov, W. (1972) *Sociolinguistic Patterns*. Philadelphia: University of Pennsylvania Press.

Salamone, F. (1976) The Arrow and the Bird: Proverbs in the Solution of Hausa Conjugal Conflicts, in *Journal of Anthropological Research*. (1976) Vol. 32, pp. 358-71.

Sanchez, M. and Blount, B.G. (ed.s) (1975) *Sociocultural Dimensions of Language use*. New York: Academic Press.

Shuy, R. and Fasold, R.W. (ed.as) (1973) *Language Attitudes: Current Trends and Prospects*.

Stross, B. (1975) Linguistic Creativity in Songs, in M. Sanchez and B.G. Blount (ed.s).

Wolfram, W. (1973) Parameters of Language Assimilation, in Shuy, R. and Fasold, R.lW. (ed.s).

What is the Russian for *Perestroika*?

Kay Richardson, University of Liverpool

Perestroika and *glasnost*, *glasnost* and *perestroika*. They will still be secure in the vocabularies of all the languages of the world long after the children of the Soviet Union and its satellites have begun to ask: 'Mummy, who was Lenin?' or for that matter: 'Mummy, who was Gorbachev?' (Keith Waterhouse, 'Just two big words', *Daily Mail* 22.8.91)

Introduction

Waterhouse, here, was writing immediately after the abortive conservative coup in the Soviet Union, August 1991. The present article is based upon work that was done before the coup, and has more to say about the meaning of *perestroika* than about the meaning of *glasnost*, those terms which according to Waterhouse have already conquered space in becoming international, and will conquer time too, by persisting through the ages to come. Like Waterhouse I am interested in the way that these words have become very generally recognised, and trying to understand a bit more clearly in both linguistic and political terms what exactly it is that has happened – and what the significance of that development might be.

Waterhouse is exaggerating, of course, and he is also oversimplifying. He appears to believe that words in general, and these ones in particular, have determinate, invariant meanings – and that is not the case. It seems that *glasnost* may be more determinate in British usage, to judge by the extent of the metaphorical usages of both terms. Both have been applied to non-Soviet affairs, but *glasnost* more than *perestroika*.

> Mr Ian MacDonald, the barrister who chaired the inquiry into the playground murder of a Manchester schoolboy, last week called for *glasnost* and power sharing to help combat racism in schools.(The *Guardian* 9.1.90)

> HOME RULE FOR GARSTON – that's the call as *perestroika* hits Liverpool. (*South Liverpool Weekly Star* 2.2.90)

Graddol, D , L. Thompson
and M. Byram (eds) (1993)
Language and Culture, Clevedon:
BAAL and Multilingual Matters

The thesis that these are now international words is one that deserves further exploration. The entry of these words into the English language was effected largely through the press. The British press produced reports upon the Soviet Union throughout the Gorbachev years. But as the ground rules of public communication there changed, so did the role of the foreign correspondents as well as the contents and the vocabulary of their reportage. The novelty of events in their eyes warranted new terms, transliterating rather than translating Gorbachev's chosen words (Service 1989: 23).

Perestroika and linguistics

Cruse (1986) argues for a contextual approach to word meaning. 'Context', for him, means, essentially, linguistic context. The meaning of a word is a function of the meaning relations it contracts in sentences of the designated language. To identify what those meaning-relations are for words of the English language he constructs sets of sentences and employs disciplined semantic intuitions – for example, on whether sentences have equivalent truth-values or not when word substitutions are carried out.

Such an approach leaves out of account the role of the *social* context in determining the meaning of a word, relegating this in effect to the domain of 'connotation' or pragmatic meaning. Cruse is also reluctant to make use of naturally-occurring sentences, favouring constructed examples. My own view is that both kinds of data are valuable: insisting on one or the other suggests a kind of methodological purism which sets method above goals. The goal of the present inquiry is to try and determine what the words *perestroika* and *glasnost* are doing in the lexicon of English. If it is true that we now have semantic intuitions about the meanings of these words, as we have about the meaning of, say, *parliament*, then only by looking at actual usage, over a period of time, will it be possible to reconstruct how those semantic intuitions could have come into being. Unless we speak Russian as well as English we can't have semantic intuitions about them based on etymology. And the press is no longer in the habit of providing glosses and definitions: that phase has passed.

Notwithstanding the problems I have just mentioned with Cruse's approach, it has one feature which is enormously important for my purposes and it is this: it becomes inappropriate, in his model, to try and draw a line between the meaning of a word, and 'encyclopaedic' facts concerning the extra-linguistic referents of the word. The arguments through which Cruse comes to this conclusion are developed in his book and I won't summarise them here. But I will use the example of *perestroika* to illustrate the point in a way that is relevant to my analysis.

Perestroika in Russian usage does not come out of nowhere. In Russian the word has its own history (see Laqueur 1989: 52). Furthermore, the morphological elements of which it is composed are still transparent in Russian, and that transparency is obviously one of the factors that allows for different interpretations in different contexts. It is possible, but difficult, to make that history count for readers of English language periodicals. English readers are even more unlikely than Russian ones to know what Stalin may have meant when he used it. And the morphology is also opaque to English readers.

Nevertheless, it is meaningful in English now and has been for several years. Newspapers used to provide glosses (*perestroika* was 'reconstruction') and more extended commentaries (The Economist 11.10.86). More important than either glossing or explicit discussion is *usage*.

To understand usage it is necessary to go back to the Soviet context and the Russian language. Even if you rely upon English translations of Russian texts, it is pretty clear that the way most Soviets used the term *perestroika* up until 1991 was as a label for what the Soviet leaders were trying to do:

> *Perestroika* is our quest to achieve a qualitatively new condition of Soviet society – politically, economically, culturally, morally, spiritually. It is a quest to bring the Soviet Union to the forefront in all of these respects. It is the renewal of socialism, a striving to reveal the truly democratic and human face of socialism. To achieve this, radical reforms must be carried out in all spheres – in our economy, social structure, psychology, and our politics, where we need democracy. (Aleksandr Yakovlev, in Cohen and Vanden Heuvel 1989: 39)

In the real world of Soviet affairs the label's referent was not singular and determinate: *perestroika* involved *goals, policies* to achieve those goals, and various *practices* which constituted the implementation of the policies. *Perestroika* uses could foreground any of these aspects or (most commonly) embrace them all. Not only that, but different members of the ruling elite (not the same set of people throughout) had different ideas about the *perestroika* project. But the important thing is that the correspondence between form (signifier) and referent was the privileged relation, rather than the relation between form and sense. The referent, for all its indeterminacy, was allowed to determine sense. Perhaps not completely: you could imagine a Russian saying 'Call this *perestroika* – nothing's been *perestroika*'d round our way' – thereby making current usage and current practice answerable to established definitions. But in general this is not what happened. In Russian the word's level of generality made that kind of critique difficult. Instead, critical comments about *perestroika* tended to be set in a hypothetical frame, allowing the leadership the right to a label of their own choosing:

> Pamyat's leader's are trying to arouse philistine sentiments among a broader segment of the population – cynical, philistine sentiments. And when they wave banners saying, 'We are for *perestroika*' a person who doesn't make careful distinctions thinks: 'Well, if that's *perestroika*, who needs it? Who wants that kind of *perestroika*?' (Aleksandr Yakovlev, in Cohen and Vanden Heuvel 1989: 66)

In English the generality problem was overlaid by the fact that the word lacks a history, as we have seen. So for us in Britain, the goal-policy-practice of *perestroika* became, even more than in Russian, the primary source of information on the word's meaning. Cruse is right that encyclopaedic knowledge cannot ultimately be separated from dictionary knowledge, for this reason: properties of the *referent*, not necessarily known when the referent was named, can become criterial in determining future uses with different referents. The question 'What does *perestroika* mean?' requires exactly the same answer as the question 'What is *perestroika*?'

Perestroika – a contested sign

So *perestroika* indexes a period in Soviet history with reference to a leadership project, and covers, variably, the goals, policies and practices associated with that project. Sovietologists certainly recognised that *perestroika* was a contested sign:

> ...like any shrewd political leader who is improvising strategy as he goes along, Gorbachev has kept manipulating the definition of that word to suit his purposes. In his hands it is a slogan for the general urge for reform, and also a label for whatever measures he chooses to implement. Sometimes, when Gorbachev is on the offensive, his *perestroika* rings with what he loves to call 'revolutionary' change; it harbors gossamer promises of democracy, of private enterprise – and it smacks of heresy to the Soviet power establishment. At other times, when Gorbachev is on the defensive, the term has more

limited, cautious connotations – of modernization, of readapting Soviet socialism without dismantling the system founded by Lenin. Then, Gorbachev uses the term *perestroika* in ways that include protection of the establishment. (Smith 1991: xvii)

Contestation certainly surrounds the goals of *perestroika*. Some, like Cohen and Vanden Heuvel (1990) see it as overturning the effects of Stalinization. Others, like Thom and Regan 1988 thought the leadership regretted only Brezhnev's stagnation, whilst there was also a fear/hope that it might involve undoing the Revolution itself. Gorbachev himself in 1990 played a wild card when he suggested that it was none of the above but something new and yet to be discovered. On the policies of *perestroika* there was more consensus. Cohen and Vanden Heuvel (1990: 15) identified five – *glasnost*, managerial decentralization, economic privatization, economic marketization and democratization. National self-determination was no part of the official agenda. The full story of the collapse of State communism in the Soviet Union and elsewhere has yet to be written.

The indeterminacy around the term *perestroika* was generated largely by political scepticism from inside and outside the Soviet Union. Sceptics doubted not only whether Gorbachev's policies could have the results that Gorbachev intended, but also whether he and his supporters meant what they said. Yet, although the policies were policies of the Soviet State, part of the desired outcome (on one interpretation) was to decrease the power of the centre. It was, in part, for others to implement *perestroika*:

> Press on, comrades – we from above, you from below. This is the only way *perestroika* can happen. Just like a vise. If there's pressure from only one side, it won't work (Gorbachev 1989, quoted in Smith 1990: 442)

Here lay the risk for the leadership, since initiatives which suited the new liberalism in the form they took, could, and did, upset the applecart in respect of their content. *Glasnost* and democratization helped produce effective, but unwelcome, nationalist movements – which had then to be portrayed as essentially anti-*perestroika* whatever they themselves said:

> There is an anti-*perestroika* minority, but it is losing its ability to profit from the old stagnant ways. Such a minority might be able to attract some people by operating under the slogans and banner of *perestroika*. We saw this in Nagorno-Karabakh, in the dispute between Armenians and Azerbaijanis, where militant nationalism paraded under the banner of *perestroika*. (Aleksandr Yakovlev, in Cohen and Vanden Heuvel 1989: 62)

The rise and fall of *perestroika*

The person who is credited with reintroducing the term *perestroika* in the 1980s is Tatyana Zaslavskaya, the author of the 1983 Novosibirsk report, which Gorbachev is supposed to have known about before he took office in 1985. During the first two years of his leadership, *perestroika* was not the keyword that it later became. Gorbachev's book *Perestroika* was first published in 1987, the year that British journalists and commentators began to use the term in their reports from the Soviet Union. At this stage the content of the term was programmatic and forward looking. All the change is to come, and no-one knows just how much change will be possible or permitted.

> For all the miles of red bunting festooning the streets of Moscow on this week's 70th anniversary of the 1917 revolution the ghosts of Communist party battles past and the threat of more fights to come spoiled the fun. Behind the scenes a Politburo split over the pace of *perestroika* (restructuring) has made Mikhail Gorbachev look suddenly vulnerable. This could not have happened at a more awkward time. Just as he was preparing to lean hard on the party to do a little restructuring of its own, Mr Gorbachev for the first time found himself having to argue the case for caution and for that most unusual of all qualities, 'revolutionary self-restraint'. (The Economist 7.11.87)

During this period of Soviet history, traditional Leninist principles still applied. The Communist party was the vanguard party, and *perestroika* was the party line. So Party members made considerable rhetorical effort to present themselves as agreeing with that line fundamentally and only disagreeing on less important questions like the pace of change.

There were more surprises in store for the Soviet leadership, and although for most users the meaning of the term *perestroika* remained tied to the policy and practices of the Soviet leadership, it also came to include the consequences of that policy and those practices. One very striking utterance by Gorbachev dates from a speech made in January 1989:

> we are only now truly understanding what *perestroika* is... the huge scale of the work to come. (quoted in Smith 1991: 78)

If that is the way the author of the policy feels about it, and most people up to that point have taken *perestroika* on his terms, the line of least resistance, then it would seem as if by 1989 the answer to the question 'what is *perestroika*, what does *perestroika*' mean?' is 'wait and see'. *Perestroika* is ongoing but not yet completed and so it is premature to try and answer the question.

Meanwhile, in Britain, the word continued to be used to refer to the Soviet leadership project, whatever it might finally have turned out to be:

> Between January and mid-November 145,000 [Russian Jews] arrived [in Israel] driven by the economic and political uncertainties of *perestroika* and the older problem of anti-Semitism. (The Guardian 10.11.90)

And so it continued, until January 1991 and the Baltic crisis. The use of force in Lithuania provoked the judgement that *perestroika* was dead, or dying, and that the Soviet Union had in effect returned to an earlier pre-*perestroika* state:

> The tanks were on the streets of Vilnius yesterday, but the political crisis they signify is in Moscow. The immediate future of Lithuanian independence is in serious doubt, but the long term future of Mr Gorbachev's *perestroika* is a much greater casualty. (The Guardian 12.1.91)

Statements declaring the end of *perestroika* only make sense when those producing them are secure in their understanding of what *perestroika* was in the first place. No longer could Gorbachev *decree* that *perestroika* continued or that it had stopped. From this point, the nature of *perestroika* had become a matter of historical record, and the leadership could be held accountable for their actions by reference to that record. As the future of the former Soviet Union became more and more uncertain, the desire to treat *perestroika* as having a fixed signification became stronger.

Conclusions

In the light of the foregoing discussion there are two points that I want to make. One is related to the question of lexical (in)determinacy, a theoretical issue, and the other, more political, is to do with the rhetoric of 'otherness' in East-West relations.

Taking the theoretical point first, the *perestroika* example can stand as an example in discussions about 'the multiaccentuality of the sign' (Voloshinov 1973). There are real limits to how far the meaning of a word can be 'reaccented'. If ever the conditions were right for doing a Humpty Dumpty and making a word mean what you choose it to mean, they were right for Gorbachev in 1987 or thereabouts. It was in his interest however to keep the meaning pretty indeterminate. That indeterminacy left space for considerable interpretative play. But hindsight shows that there

were some changes which it could not encompass. It did not prove
indeterminate enough to provide support for the anti-democratic
use of troops in the rebellious republics, it could not encompass the
disestablishment of the Communist party, or the break-up of the
Soviet Union itself.

As for the political significance of this case study, in a Western
context, the point to make here is that the choice of a Russian
word rather than the English 'restructuring' can be usefully set in
the context of the rhetorics of international relations. In the
rhetoric of East-West relations, the Cold War discourse long
dominated representations. In the Cold War discourse the enemy
was as unlike 'us' as it was possible to be. Hawks in the American
administration were haunted by 'the spectre of moral
equivalence', by which they meant a tendency in the peace
movement to speak (wrongly) as if the crimes of the two
superpowers put their respective regimes on a morally equal
footing. Even as the Cold War discourse was losing its grip upon
our understanding, during Gorbachev's *perestroika*, there was
room to play up the similarities between Western and Soviet
society or to play up the differences, according to ideological
preference. A consensus developed that *glasnost* and *perestroika*
were untranslatable terms. The resources of English permitted
circumlocutory descriptions of what *glasnost* and *perestroika*
were, but not one-word synonyms. This carries the implication
that the societies themselves were non-comparable. A special
term was required because the process itself was so
unprecedented and so bound up with the nature of a Soviet-style
command economy.

Thus, at one level, the use of the term *perestroika* in preference
to a more familiar expression underlines the prevailing view that
Soviet and Western societies are non-comparable. But
comparability is a matter of textual rhetoric generally and not just
of individual words. When Gorbachev compared *perestroika* with
Lenin's New Economic Policy, and Shevardnadze compared it
with Roosevelt's New Deal they were not disagreeing with one
another. But in the latter comparison we can see a desire to
undermine the rhetoric of difference. The New Deal was of course
an interventionist form of social reconstruction, perceivable
therefore as socialism introduced to moderate the effects of
capitalism. At the same time however it would serve as a
reminder to Westerners, especially Americans, that they too had
had crises which had necessitated extra-ordinary measures by
way of remedy.

As a final point, consider what the metaphorical uses of *glasnost* and *perestroika* mentioned at the beginning of this article suggest, regarding the comparability of Western and Soviet society. For writers who employ *perestroika* as a metaphor, the point is to represent British institutions as undemocratic, secretive, sclerotically bureaucratic. These are institutions where *perestroika* can be implemented. Thus, although such comparisons undermine the virtue of our society, they do so by reinscribing the vice of the enemy's. Sometimes we are no better than they.

References

Cruse, D. A. (1986) *Lexical semantics* Cambridge: Cambridge University Press

Cohen, S. and Vanden Heuvel, K. (1989) *Voices of glasnost* London: W. W. Norton

Gorbachev, M. (1987) *Perestroika: new thinking for our country and the world*. London: Fontana

Laqueur, Walter (1989) *The long road to freedom: Russia and glasnost. London*: Unwin Hyman

Service, R. (1989) 'Mikhail Gorbachev as a political reformer'. In R. J. Hill and J. A. Dellenbrant (eds.) *Gorbachev and Perestroika: towards a new socialism* London: Edward Elgar

Smith, H. (1990) *The new Russians* London: Hutchinson

Thom, F. and Regan, D. (1988) *Gorbachev, glasnost and Lenin: behind the new thinking* London: Policy Research Publications

Voloshinov, V. N. (1973) *Marxism and the philosophy of language.* London: Seminar Press (first published 1930)

Young, M. J. and Launer, M. K. (1991) 'Redefining *glasnost* in the Soviet media: the recontextualization of Chernobyl'. *Journal of Communication* **41 – 2**: 102-124

Dialogic Relationships and the Construction of Knowledge in Children's Informal Talk

Janet Maybin, Open University

Introduction: the situatedness of language and the centrality of dialogue

The view of language as a socially and culturally situated activity, mediating between the cognitive development of the individual on the one hand and that individual's cultural and historical environment on the other (Vygotsky 1978), has proved particularily fruitful to researchers interested in the role of dialogue in children's learning. Many of these have focused on child-adult conversations, in educational or other directed learning contexts. The adult function of 'scaffolding' children's learning through talk is seen as centrally important to their conceptual development (eg Bruner (1985), Wells (1985), Edwards and Mercer (1987)). And because this talk is contextualized in particular kinds of relationships and social contexts, these shape and influence the nature of meanings and knowledge internalised by individual children. Cognitive development is therefore inseparable from the processes of socialisation into a particular culture.

Less well researched is the area of children's informal talk, when children rather than adults are taking a leading conversational role. I shall use Vygotsky's ideas about the cultural contextualisation of language, and about the importance of focusing on dialogue rather than on individual utterances, to look at and examine some of the ways in which knowledge and identities are being constructed in these contexts. In order to examine the different layers of meaning in the children's talk, I shall also draw on ideas from the writings of Bakhtin and Volosinov, focusing particularily on the dialogic relationships between and within utterances. My data comes from contexts which would not normally be described as learning situations, but I shall argue that some very important learning is indeed

Graddol, D , L. Thompson
and M. Byram (eds) (1993)
Language and Culture, Clevedon:
BAAL and Multilingual Matters

occurring, concerning personal relationships, social institutions and cultural values.

My own data was collected using radio microphones and small personal cassette recorders from 10-12 year olds in two middle schools serving council estates in a new town in south east England. I chose this age-group because they are moving from childhood into adolescence, and are therefore likely to be developing and negotiating new kinds of cultural knowledge and personal identities. In the first school I focused mainly on one ten year old girl, collecting all her talk (and the talk of those within her hearing) over three days from 8.45am when she arrived in the classroom, to 3.00pm when she finished school. In the second school I spent three weeks recording two groups of friends – three boys and three girls. In both schools I collected additional material from other children in the class, and carried out extensive interviews with children about issues cropping up on the tapes, and about their own personal interests.

One of my major findings is that, through the dialogic relationships between and within utterances, children's negotiation of meanings and knowledge is carried on simultaneously at a number of different levels. This only becomes apparent through carefully scrutinising long continuous stretches of recorded talk.

Dialogic relationships and the taking on of voices

Vygotsky's ideas about the situatedness of language, and about the way in which the meanings of words and phrases are tied up with the cultural contexts of their use, are developed further in the writings of Bakhtin and Volosinov. They approach language not as a set of tools which can be manipulated to serve individual cognitive and social ends, but as ideologically and culturally saturated behaviour, emerging from particular patterns of social relationship and political structure.

They suggest that any utterance is multiply contextualized, through various different kinds of dialogic relationships. In terms of external dialogic relationships, an utterance reflects not only the intention of the person producing it, but also the voices to whom it is addressed, and previous voices it has heard. It is always part of a chain of utterances, both within a current conversation, and in relation to previous conversations in other contexts. The internal dialogic relationships within an utterance are set up, according to Bakhtin, because we essentially talk with other people's voices and other people's words, and that these bring with them into an utterance the meanings and nuances from previous speakers, and from other contexts .

> Language is not a neutral medium which passes freely and easily into the private property of the speaker's intentions; it is populated – overpopulated, with the intentions of others' (Bakhtin 1981:294).

When we invoke a speaker's voice this brings with it what Bakhtin calls a particular 'social language', that is, a discourse associated with a specific stratum of society, for example a profession or age-group, within a given social system at a particular time. These social languages shape what people can and can't say, because they encapsulate particular social relationships and cultural values. Social languages are associated with what Bakhtin calls 'speech genres', which are used in particular situations, and involve typical forms of utterance, expression and themes. Social languages and speech genres are often interlinked. In my research, for example, the subject matter and vocabulary used in a conversation which is taking place in the girls' school cloakroom reflects both their age-group and gender (and probably class), and also the context of that particular social interaction (Maybin 1991).

Bakhtin suggests that a voice can be taken on directly, without acknowledgement, so that speakers act as if that voice were their own. On the other hand, speakers can also explicitly quote themselves and other people, through the use of reported speech. Bakhtin points out that in conversation reported speech is seldom reproduced accurately, unless it comes from a particularily authoritative voice, but is manufactured to fit in with the speaker's current conversational intentions. Often one can hear the voice of the speaker behind the manufactured voice which they are reporting, in the same way as one perceives a novelist's use of irony in the particular words ascribed to one of their fictional characters.

The using of other people's voices within an utterance has to be seen within the context of Bakhtin's view of language as involving a central tension between centripetal and centrifugal forces, the first associated with socio-political centralization and a relatively inflexible 'authoritative discourse', and the second with the stratification and diversification of various social languages, and with a more provisional, interactive 'inwardly persuasive discourse'. Within any one utterance, there will be evidence of the struggle between these two opposing forces.

Examples of children's dialogue

At first impression, the meanings in any particular snatch of children's conversation often seem ambiguous or provisional, a kind of unfinished attempt at negotiating shared understanding. Interpretation of an individual child's contributions may depend on the nature of the response from other participants in the conversation, and where there is disagreement this is often left unresolved. I have argued elsewhere that this very provisionality makes children's conversations a rich site for learning (Maybin 1991). Viewed in its historical context, the negotiation of meaning appears less haphazard and arbitrary. Listening to long stretches of continuous data covering a number of days one begins to notice how particular themes and topics resurface in different conversational contexts, to be explored and tackled by children in ways which acknowledge and build on their previous related conversations and shared experience. The context of any conversation thus includes these previous conversations, which contribute additional layers of meaning to the immediate exchange. These more extended dialogic relationships seem to be part of what I shall term 'long conversations', which are carried on intermittently across days and weeks and are which are about social values and personal positionings. In order to understand a particular interchange between children, I would suggest that one needs to have some knowledge of the 'long conversations', to which this contributes.

As well as being multi-layered in a historical sense, conversations are made more complex by the way children introduce other contexts through their invocation of additional voices, particularily in reported speech. I shall explain in more detail how these different kinds of links and references work, in relation to the specific examples of data below.

I will look first at an example which shows how links across conversations bring additional layers of meaning to a particular interchange. The immediate subject matter of the girls' conversation below is a dispute over what was said in a previous conversation, and this is never really resolved. However at another level the topic is to do with friendship, which has been explored in various related ways in previous conversations.

Jenny, Angie and Kerry are working together to mount their findings from a scavenging hunt on a display sheet. Kerry has just left their table for a few minutes.

(The use of '/' indicates interrupted speech˙ and any additional information is placed in brackets eg (laughter))).

Jenny: I'm going to tell Kerry.
Angie: What?
Jenny: That we said we were going to ignore her.
Angie: I never said that, you did.
Jenny: Yea, you did as well, you did as well.
Angie: I said just to pretend that she's not there.
Jenny: Yea, that's still saying to ignore.
Angie: I was the one who thought of it/
Jenny: /no I was the one who thought of it/
Angie: /and you went along. (To Kerry, who has just returned to the table) Right, we were going to pretend that we couldn't see you, right. And just now when I says that she never thought of it, but I thought of it, right and then she went along with it. (pause) I'm, sorry, Kerry.
Kerry: It's alright. I like a good joke, anyway.

The argument over who said what and what they meant by it seems to be of considerable importance to Jenny and Angie; but much is left unresolved. Is ignoring someone the same as pretending they're not there, or pretending not to see them? Who is responsible for the act of 'telling' Kerry: Jenny who said she was going to, or Angie who did it? And who was responsible for hatching the plan? Had Angie and Jenny really meant to be nasty to Kerry, and, if so, did Kerry realise this when she redefined their intentions as 'a good joke'? These alternatives are all possible interpretations, and may be drawn on selectively by any of the three girls in future conversations.

This interchange illustrates the provisionality of meaning which seems to characterize so much of children's informal talk, when viewed in its immediate context. But I would suggest that the talk also needs to be set within the context of other previous conversations in my recordings about 'breaking up with' friends, 'using' people, 'telling on' people, and 'going along with' something. In this sense it is part of the long conversation about what constitutes friendly and unfriendly behaviour, and about the finer distinctions involved in apportioning blame and responsibility for each other's actions which is being carried on between children on various different occasions, in relation to their own developing social competencies and personhood. Jenny, Angie and Kerry aren't just talking to and listening to each other in the present conversation; they are also hearing, and responding to, their own and other voices from previous conversational contexts.

Having discussed the links between conversations across time,

I shall look now at how additional layers of meaning are created within an exchange between speakers by the calling up of different voices through reported speech. In my data children's anecdotes were related almost entirely through reported dialogue, so that they created a kind of conversation within a conversation, thus setting up a new layer of dialogic relationships. The next example, (which also occurred while mounting the scavenging findings), shows Julie and Kirsty worrying about the amount of swearing on the tapes I am collecting.

Julie   Children aren't meant to swear
Kirsty   If people swear at them, they can swear back
Julie: I swore at my mum the other day because she started, she hit me.
Kirsty: What did you do?
Julie: I swore at my mum, I says `I'm packing my cases and I don't care what you say' and she goes `Ooh?' and (I go) `yea!'.I'm really cheeky to my mother.

This anecdote creates, as it were, a short sidetrack from Julie and Kirsty's conversation, a space within which to explore a particular idea in a bit more detail. On one level the anecdote provides a conversational turn in relation to the question of when it is permissable to swear. Julie is responding to Kirsty's statement that if people swear at you, then you can swear back. She says she only swore at her mother under extreme provocation; her mother hit her and she felt like leaving home. But, she adds, this is still being 'really cheeky'.

The anecdote however is not just about when to swear. Julie's use of the formulaic phrase 'I'm packing my cases' invokes a scenario within which to play out particular aspects of her relationship with her mother, a recurring theme in conversations with friends. And the story will be heard by Kirsty in the context of other friends' anecdotes about the ways mothers and daughters treat each other, and further picaresque stories about questioning and resisting adult authority. This use of reported speech creates a 'theme within a theme' (Volosinov 1973), which sets up a dialogue with the original conversation theme (both are part of broader discussions concerning issues of power and authority, and the cultural appropriateness of particular kinds of language behaviour), and with other previous conversations. Meaning is thus shaped both by the particular histories and relationships of individual girls, and by the intersection of these with broader cultural themes.

In reporting her mother's speech, Julie is not expected by her listeners to reproduce her mother's words exactly as she heard them. She in fact manufactures a voice for her mother, to fit in with the purpose of the story. Volosinov suggests that the relationship between the author's voice, and those of the characters they create, can be manipulated in quite complex ways, depending on the author's intentions. In the next example, Darren also manufactures his own, and a man's voice, in an anecdote told while children are queueing in the playground, waiting to go in to lunch. There was a lot of noise and milling about in the queue, and anecdotes told in this context needed to be extremely arresting and lively in order to hold their audience. At this point, one child has just sworn at another.

Martie: I said that to a real man and he went, he went `dick head' [and I
         went] `of course I am!' (laughter) And he goes `erm!' (growling
         and laughter)
Darren: This man called me a fucking bastard, right, I go `back to you', he
         goes `come here', I go `come on, then' and he's got about size 10
         trainers and he chased me, right, and then when he got, he
         catched me, right, like that, and he goes `who's fucking saying?'
         And I goes `fuck off', I says `fuck off' and he goes, he goes, `Do you
         want a fight?' I go `not tonight, darling' and he goes `piss off!'

In the boys' conversations they often seem to be jostling for position, capping each other's comments with a more impressive contribution. Here, Darren's story is a response to Martie's rather abbreviated anecdote. It is more developed, the man is more frightening, and the turnaround at the end more dramatic and ingenious. As well as providing a turn in the immediate conversation, it also contributes to a recurring theme in the boys' talk concerning their toughness and canniness, which are important aspects of the way they present themselves to each other. And it echoes the concern of Julie's anecdote about how far adult authority can, and should be, contested.

Within the dialogue, Darren, like Julie, uses reported dialogue to tell his story. But Darren doesn't just create voices for himself and the man. He also, inside the story, at the point when things are getting really alarming, portrays himself as taking on a different voice ('not tonight, darling'). Darren adopts a slightly higher pitched voice at this point, portraying what could be either a woman or a homosexual man rejecting a partner's advances. The use of this voice, as in Julie's 'I'm packing my cases', invokes a particular scenario or scenarios with associated relationships.

As Bakhtin (1986) points out, the taking on of another voice sets up dialogues between the various voices invoked in an utterance, and between these voices and the speaker's intentions. In

Darren's case, calling up the speech genre of another context changes the relationship between himself and the man in a way which defuses the situation through humour, and signals a kind of submission which still enables him to maintain face rather more successfully than Martie did in his story. This is his internal intention, as it were, within the (possibly fictional) context of the anecdote. There is also his intention as a speaker following, and hoping to decisively cap, Martie's anecdote, and the manufacture of voices within the anecdote needs to be seen in relation to this conversational aim. There is thus a complex nesting of different conversational contexts: from the long conversation concerning canniness and resisting authority, to Darren's and Martie's conversation, to the reported interchange between Martie and the man, to the scenario invoked by 'not tonight, darling'. And particular dialogic relationships, as Bakhtin suggests, cut across those various different contexts.

The next example also shows children manufacturing their own and other people's voices. First, Sarah assumes the concerned voice of a naive mother who thinks her daughter's bruises have come from fighting, and, secondly, Geoffrey provides an ironic parody of his own voice in order to clarify a misunderstanding. This conversation occurs while the children were queueing in the school corridor, waiting for the coach to arrive which would   take them swimming. Darren has just pretended to give Sherri a love bite.

Sherri:	(laughing) My mum thinks I've been in fights again!
Sarah:	What do your mum go? `Who gave you a big bruise?' (laughter)
Terry:	I'll give her a double bruise, aha!
Darren:	I gave her one on the arm

....

Geoffrey:	Oi, you could never give someone a lovebite on the arm, could you, could you? You can't!
Sherri:	You can, if you've got a T-shirt on.
Geoffrey:	Yea I mean, look, it's really exciting look, let's get down to there, next time it'll be your finger! (noise of kissing).

Geoffrey is driven to the use of irony here to explain to Sherri that he was not asking whether it was physically possible to bite an arm, but whether it was culturally appropriate. He puts on an excited enthusiastic voice to show just how ridiculous such enthusiasm would be. Volosinov suggests that in the use of irony we can hear two voices simultaneously, the author's and the manufactured voice, and that the interplay between these conveys a range of possible meanings. We are aware of Geoffrey's authorial voice mocking his own exaggerated' parody, which he clearly frames ('Yes, I mean, look...') as a special performance. (Some features of these 'manufactured' voices are inevitably lost in the written medium).

Both Vygotsky and Bakhtin suggest that conversations are internalised to become inner dialogues. Thus, individual thought processes also involve the taking on of voices, which provide responses to voices heard in previous conversations, and which call up particular relationships and contexts. The last extract comes from an interview with two girls, Karlie and Nicole. Karlie had explained that she sometimes goes to visit her Dad in prison, and I asked her what it was like doing that. Karlie answers me by representing her feelings at the prison as an inner dialogue, which involves invoking her own voice as if she were talking first to herself, and then to her dad.

Karlie   It's like – it's just loads and loads of bars. So you think 'What's my dad doing in here, he didn't do nothing' because he got accused by chopping someone's hand off so- and it weren't true,........and you get in there, and you're seeing him, and you think 'Come with us, come with us, you can't stay in here cause it's not true really, is it?' so you think 'You can come with us now, you can get out, but it's just not true'.

When I was trying to punctuate this transcribed talk with speech marks, it was difficult to make out where one voice ends and another starts, or to identify particular audiences. Sometimes Karlie seems to be addressing herself, sometimes her father, sometimes myself and sometimes previous voices she has heard. It's difficult to know, for example, to whom her final 'it's just not true' is addressed, and whether it refers to the crime of which her father is accused or to the possibility of taking him home with her, or to both. The fragmented nature of the dialogues invoked in Karlie's response to my question would suggest that her talk here is close to what Vygotsky calls 'inner speech', where dialogues we have had, and those which we might have with other people, feed into our internal thought processes. I would suggest that this example also shows how the voices and dialogues with which we think are themselves rooted and contextualized in particular cultural contexts, with associated social values and relationships.

This utterance then has its own internal business: Karlie is struggling to come to terms with her father's imprisonment, and positioning herself in relation to the differing accounts of his guilt. She is also, at the level of my interview conversation with her, using this representation of her inner dialogue to convey a particular presentation of herself, to me. The voices she invokes are therefore also shaped and influenced by considerations relating to the interview context , and to her relationship with me, and with her friend Nicole.

Conclusion

I have argued that in order to understand how children are constructing knowledge in their informal talk, we need to look at the historical and contemporary contextualization of their conversations. One way of doing this is to examine the dialogic relationships between and within utterances, which are often invoked through the use of reported speech and through the taking on of voices. An important way in which any particular conversation is contextualized is in terms of its contribution to what I have called 'long conversations', which are going on between children over days and weeks about various social values and personal positionings. Conversations also involve the calling up of a number of different contexts which operate simultaneously within the talk, so that meanings can pertain to a number of alternative, but often overlapping, frames of reference. This multi-layering of contextual frames adds complexity to the interpretative possibilities, both in creating alternative contexts within which to explore and experiment with a particular meaning, and in setting up additional dialogic relations between the voices across these different contexts. Meanings are thus being continually questioned and challenged in children's conversations, and in the extension of these conversations towards 'inner speech'. The examination of long stretches of continuous data begins to expose the ways in which the multiple contextualization of utterances in children's informal talk mediates between their construction of knowledge and personhood on the one hand, and their socialization into a particular cultural and historical environment on the other.

References

Bakhtin, M. M. (1981) *The dialogic imagination: four essays by M. M. Bakhtin..* (ed. M. Holquist).Austin: University of Texas Press.

Bakhtin, M. M. (1986) *Speech genres and other late essays* (ed. Caryl Emerson and Michael Holquist). Austin: University of Texas Press.

Bruner, J. (1985) Vygotsky: a cultural and historical perspective. In J. Wertsch (ed) *Culture, Communication and Cognition: Vygotskian perspectives.* Cambridge: Cambridge University Press.

Edwards, D. and Mercer, N. (1987) *Common Knowledge: the development of understanding in the classroom* . London: Methuen.

Maybin, J. (1991) Children's informal talk and the construction of meaning, *English in Education,.*25, 34 – 49.

Voloshinov, V. N. (1973) *Marxism and the Philosophy of Language.* (trans. L. Matejka and I. R. Titunik). New York: Seminar Press.

Vygotsky, L. (1978) *Mind in Society: the development of higher psychological processes..* (ed. Cole, M. et al). Cambridge: Harvard University Press.

Wells, G. (1985) *Language at Home and at School.* Cambridge: Cambridge University Press.

I would like to thank Brian Street and Gemma Moss for comments on an earlier draft of this paper.